The Equality Duty for Educational Professionals

A simple guide to producing your Single Equality Plans

Geraldine Hills

INCLUSIVE CHOICE

Inclusive Choice Consultancy

22 Baldock Road, Manchester, M20 6JG

www.inclusivechoice.com

First published 2011

This book is intended to provide general guidance on the law. It does not constitute legal advice and is not an authoritative treatment of the law. Professional advice should be sought before acting on any of the material contained in this book as it may not be appropriate to your circumstances. This book is not intended to be used in place of reading the Codes of Practice or the Equality Act (2010).

ISBN: 978-1-4709-3978-6

To Lavern Ritch
For all that you were and all that you should have been.
To Sam for all that you are.

"The sun showers light to one and all without any discrimination. Similarly, humans should also engage themselves in doing works for the benefit of the society."

Atharva Veda

CONTENTS

ABOUT THE AUTHOR

Geraldine Hills is the founder and director of Inclusive Choice Consultancy. She has been working with people with disabilities for many years in various capacities.

She holds a BA in Learning Disability Studies from the Victoria University of Manchester, and is a frequent guest lecturer in the education department at Manchester University.

Geraldine has experience of the Special Educational Needs and Disability Tribunal as a parent who successfully won a tribunal for her child.

She runs many courses for Manchester City Council as well as other local authorities and also works in collaboration with associated services such as parent partnership, educational psychologists, and statutory assessment teams. She works as a consultant and trainer in the implementation of the Equality Duty in schools.

Other published books by Geraldine Hills:

"The Equality Act for Educational Professionals: A Simple Guide to Disability Inclusion in Schools", Routledge, 2011.

"A Parents' Guide to Disability Discrimination and Their Child's Education"
`www.inclusivechoice.com`

HOW TO USE THIS BOOK

This book has concentrated on disability equality, since this is the most complex to implement. However, I have also included explanations and examples of race and gender equality issues as well as an example single equality scheme that also address these issues. Although this book is predominantly concerned with the Disability Equality Duty (DED) it is important that you remember to pay 'due regard' to your equality duties for all protected groups especially when reviewing any current or future policy and practice.

At the end of most sections, there is a list of documents and booklets that are available from the website that accompanies this book. These can be found at `www.inclusivechoice.com`, and are free to download. You will also find on the website details of courses and INSET training for your school. This book contains many worked examples and case studies for discussion.

PREFACE

Never has it been more important than now to help shape our society.

Parents and teachers are the ones that can bring about change. You are the ones that can *be the change you want to see.* Malcolm Gladwell's book, The Tipping Point, states

> "If you want to bring about change in peoples beliefs and behaviour, a change that would persist and serve as an example to others you need to create communities around them, where those new beliefs could be practiced and expressed and nurtured."

By becoming the change you want to see in your school, you are creating that positive example that will go on to promote a caring, tolerant, respectful and inclusive school, and bring about cohesion in our communities.

In a recent report *"Equality duty and schools lessons for the future"* produced by the Equality and Human Rights Commission (EHRC), when schools were asked to give an example of equality work from the duties, they rarely identified tackling prejudice-related bullying, exclusions or stereotyping.

The EHRC believes this may be due to a number of factors, including lack of awareness of these issues, a belief that equality means ensuring that activities are 'open' to all pupils rather than actively challenging disadvantage, or because schools prefer to address issues which appear to be easier to tackle. It also suggests that schools' approach to equality work may not be evidence-led.

To get a complete picture, it is important to take a systematic approach to collecting, analysing, and interpreting data. This will allow your school to find useful evidence on how you are doing in regard to equality duties.

Here's what you already know:
- The importance of improving outcomes for all protected groups that the Equality Duty covers.
- You need facts in order to produce meaningful equality documents.
- You need a clear sense of who the drivers are for equality work in your school.

But do you know?
- What your school's strengths and weaknesses are in your equality duties?
- If you are building on them?
- Is your school positive about achieving them?
- Does it show?

If you can answer these questions positively then you are on the way to having a truly inclusive school. If you celebrate your strengths by building on them and being open about your weaknesses and improving on them, then you are well on your way to becoming a remarkable school.

In my book "The Equality Act for Educational Professionals" I discuss the importance of a full understanding of the Equality Act, and your duties to make reasonable adjustments for pupils with SEN and disabilities. Asking yourself key questions about your school's approach to inclusion can help you uncover any gaps in your knowledge of the Equality Act.

Don't forget the things that you do every day that can make such a difference to pupils with disabilities. It may be being aware of your language, having disability awareness in your curriculum, buddy schemes, or involvement of parents of pupils with disabilities. These small things can lead to long term changes.

Apply an *appreciative inquiry* into all that you do in your school. Applying this concept will ensure that you get used to recognising good practice from staff and pupils alike. Don't look for what is broken and fix it, rather look at what works.

Trust yourself. It's OK to make mistakes. Accept them and learn from them. Don't think that you've got to know all the answers, or that you must have an entire plan laid out in advance. Have the guts to ask the hard questions. Nobody get its right all the time but by sharing and talking about mistakes you will create an open, transparent and trustworthy school.

In the words of Michael Jordan: "I've missed more than 9000 shots in my career. I've lost almost 300 games. 26 times, I've been trusted to take the game winning shot and missed. I've failed over and over and over again in my life. And that is why I succeed."

Break down any old schemas your school might have and replace them with a schema that reflects your school ethos and commitment to promote equality. Look for any complacency - *"we've always done it this way"* - and change your line of thinking. Be remarkable in your approach towards pupils with disabilities and their families. Let's not just regurgitate the facts about successful inclusion in our schools, let's figure out the point of it all.

Closing the knowledge gap

I had the unfortunate experience of taking my son's previous school to tribunal for discriminating against him, which the judge found in my favour. It was the most difficult and emotional journey I have ever been on in my life. After the case was over I started thinking about what mistakes the school had made, and why it had ended in a parent feeling they had no choice but to go to tribunal.

The importance of quality training can never be underestimated, especially when it come to closing knowledge gaps. To this day is saddens me that the vice-chair of governors chose to become defensive and hostile towards me. It was that attitude, that lack of training, and unwillingness to find a solution and work alongside others that caused him to advise the head-teacher wrongly. It gave me no pleasure to win the case, as it was so unnecessary, when all that was needed was a discussion about what reasonable adjustments could have been made, and who the school could have worked with and consulted.

The number of SEN tribunals has risen by 64% in 12 years, and by 16% since 2008[1]. A significant number of these were against schools, where parents brought about a claim of disability discrimination as laid down by the Equality Act. It doesn't have to be like this. The sad reality is that many of these cases could have been avoided if only the schools had had a better understanding of the Equality Act and their duties toward pupils with disabilities.

Sometimes it can be our own attitudes and beliefs that are prejudiced, and need adjusting. Whether you are a teacher or a parent, admitting that you may need to change your own behaviour or thoughts can be a good start to building community cohesion in our schools.

Reasonable Adjustments

The good news, for most schools at least, is that you are implementing reasonable adjustments every day, maybe without even knowing it! A reasonable adjustment doesn't have to be something that is done on a grand scale, or that costs lots of money. It can be in the little things you do every day, such as placing a hearing impaired child at the front of the class, or asking a parent what sort of things they do at home to help their child. It could be asking the pupil what makes things easier for them, thinking about lighting, the language you use or adjusting your own attitude.

The attitude of staff is fundamental to achieving successful outcomes for pupils with disabilities. Where staff are positive and demonstrate a 'can-do' approach, barriers are more easily overcome. Having a proactive approach to reasonable adjustments and finding creative ways to overcome potential barriers will go a long way to achieving better outcomes for children with disabilities. Schools have identified more effective reasonable adjustments by actively identifying barriers as early as possible and exploring solutions using a practical, problem-solving approach.

The changes you make for pupils with disabilities can make your school a better place for other pupils too. The best change you can make in your school to include children with disabilities is in the attitudes of the staff and other pupils. Improving that will make your school a much better place for all children.

Are you mediocre or remarkable?

Mediocrity has many guises - "good enough", average, functioning at grade level, proficient, on target. When it comes to reasonable adjustments be careful not to fall in to a

---

[1] Times Educational Supplement, 30 July, 2010

mediocre line of thinking so that your reasonable adjustments do nothing more than skim the surface of creating real change in your school that has an overall benefit to your school.

Sometimes it can be our own attitudes and beliefs that are prejudiced, and need adjustment. Discrimination can only be avoided in our schools if we are willing to accept that no matter how good our intentions are, we may have ideas or beliefs about disability that may cause us to treat pupils with disabilities differently however unintentionally.

Being noticed is not the same as being remarkable. Running down the street naked will get you noticed, but it won't accomplish much. It's easy to pull off a stunt, but not useful. Are you a remarkable teacher? Is your school remarkable? What is remarkable, different or unusual about your approach towards inclusion?

An example of being remarkable is the head-teacher Anne Hughes who introduced a Rights Respecting framework at Knights Enham junior school, and subsequently became the first school in the world to be awarded a UNICEF level 2 Rights Respecting School Award. The staff and pupils of the schools have been remarkable in their determination to adopt this framework.

Sometimes it is a little frightening to dive in, sometimes it is hard to get over what you used to do and try doing things in a new way. The next time you are faced with issues around inclusion, whether you're the parent or the teacher, what creative and constructive reasonable adjustment could you come up with that would make you stand out from the crowd and become remarkable? Do something remarkable. Be remarkable in your relationships with the parent, teacher or pupils.

"If you cannot do great things, do small things in a great way"

Napoleon Hills (American author)

Inclusive Choice

Inclusive Choice provides training for schools and parents across the UK in the Equality Act and equality duties. Information about these courses can be found at `www.inclusivechoice.com`. My new book *"The Equality Act for Educational Professionals"* for schools can be found at Amazon. I have also written a free book for parents *"A parent's guide to Disability Discrimination and their child's education"* which can be downloaded from the website.

JARGON BUSTING

Acronyms are sometimes used to exclude people by talking in a way that only some people know what is being said. If we want to be inclusive then we need to use inclusive language that everyone can understand. Try to use acronyms and jargon as little as possible; however it is inevitable that they will be used in everyday conversation, and so here are some definitions…

EA	Equality Act
DDA	Disability Discrimination Act
SENDA	Special Educational Needs and Disability Act
SEND	Special Educational Needs and Disability (Tribunal)
DED	Disability Equality Duty
DES	Disability Equality Scheme
SED	Single Equality Duty
PSED	Public Sector Equality Duty
EHRC	Equality and Human Rights Commission
IPSEA	Independent Parental Special Educational Advice
DPA	Data Protection Act

 INTRODUCTION

BACKGROUND TO DISABILITY EQUALITY AND THE DED

In this section we look at how the Disability Equality Duty came about, and the legislation that it is based on. The DED is about making your school a better place for people with disabilities. It is built upon the Disability Discrimination Act (and the later Equality Act) which set down in law how you must treat people with disabilities in everyday school life.

Although this book is predominantly concerned with your Disability Equality Duty, this is only one section of your equality duties and when you are planning and revising your equality schemes you must apply the same consideration to your Race Equality Duty (RED) and Gender Equality Duty (GED). However, disability equality is often the most complex to implement, and so this book concentrates on that.

Disability Equality Schemes

The Disability Discrimination Act (2005) introduced the Equality Duty. This required all public bodies, including schools, to produce a "Disability Equality Scheme". The Equality Act (2010) relaxes this requirement so that bodies with fewer than 150 employees no longer have to produce a "scheme". However, all public bodies still need to publish a package of documents. I have chosen to continue to call this package of documents your Disability Equality Scheme, since to invent another name for it would just increase confusion.

Does my school need to have a single equality policy?

Your school may well have moved from having three separate schemes: disability, race and gender, to a Single Equality Scheme. If you decide to produce a single equality scheme, you need to ensure that you meet the requirements of the race, disability and gender equality duties. Schools are legally permitted to continue to publish separate equality documents or to combine them into a separate document – a single equality duty.

It is important that you remember each of the requirements of each equality duty will need to be separately met and evidenced in a clearly identifiable way, either within your single scheme or within your three separate schemes. There should be no assumption that application of any arrangements, which meet one general duty, will meet all of them, as the requirements are slightly different.

What are the public sector duties?

The Equality Act (2010) brings in a new duty called the Public Sector Equality Duty. Public bodies – from government departments to local authorities, schools, health bodies and police authorities – are required to adhere to this duty.

The equality duties cover race, gender, and disability, but also require organisations to consider equality issues regarding age, sexuality, trans-gender, religion, and maternity.

Under the new Duty, public bodies must think about how they stop *discrimination, harassment,* and *victimisation* of people who share a protected characteristic. The protected characteristics are:

- **Age.** Where this is referred to, it refers to a person belonging to a particular age. (e.g. 32 year olds) or range of ages (e.g. 18 - 30 year olds).
- **Disability.** A person has a disability if s/he has a physical or mental impairment which has a substantial and long-term adverse effect on that person's ability to carry out normal day-to-day activities.
- **Gender reassignment.** The process of transitioning from one gender to another.
- **Marriage and civil partnership.** Marriage is defined as a 'union between a man and a woman'. Same-sex couples can have their relationships legally recognised as

'civil partnerships'. Civil partners must be treated the same as married couples on a wide range of legal matters.

- **Pregnancy and maternity.** Pregnancy is the condition of being pregnant or expecting a baby. Maternity refers to the period after the birth, and is linked to maternity leave in the employment context. In the non-work context, protection against maternity discrimination is for 26 weeks after giving birth, and this includes treating a woman unfavourably because she is breastfeeding.
- **Race.** Refers to a group of people defined by their race, colour, and nationality (including citizenship) ethnic or national origins.
- **Religion and belief.** Religion has the meaning usually given to it but belief includes religious and philosophical beliefs including lack of belief (e.g. Atheism). Generally, a belief should affect your life choices or the way you live for it to be included in the definition.
- **Gender.** A man or a woman.
- **Sexual orientation.** Whether a person's sexual attraction is towards their own sex, the opposite sex or to both sexes.

Discrimination means treating people unfairly because of their protected characteristic.

Harassment covers a wide range of offensive behaviour. It is commonly understood as behaviour intended to disturb or upset, and it is characteristically repetitive. In the legal sense, it is intentional behaviour, which is found threatening or disturbing

Victimisation means treating people unfairly or badly because they complained about discrimination or harassment.

You must think about how to give different people equal chances in your school. You must also think about how to "Foster good relations between people who share a protected characteristic and those who do not".

You are required to demonstrate that your school is taking action on race, disability and gender equality in policy-making, the delivery of services and employment.

The duties mean that you have to take action to deliver better outcomes for people of different racial groups, people with disabilities and men and women, including transsexual men and women. The duties require you to take steps not just to eliminate unlawful discrimination and harassment, but also to actively promote equality.

Although this book is predominantly concerned with your Disability Equality Duty, there is a brief section on race/ethnicity and gender equality duties.

HISTORY OF RECENT DISABILITY LEGISLATION

Figure 1 shows a timeline of recent equality legislation.

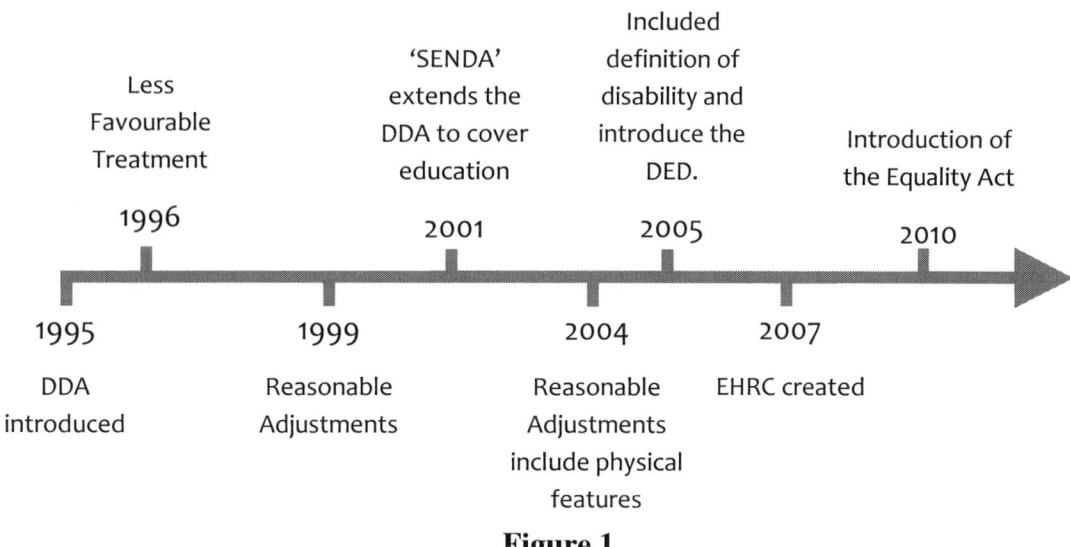

Figure 1

The Disability Discrimination Act (1995) departed from the fundamental principles of older UK discrimination law (the Sex Discrimination Act 1975 and the Race Relations Act 1976). Previous Acts depended on the concepts of "direct discrimination" and "indirect discrimination". However, these concepts are insufficient to deal with the issues of disability discrimination.

The core concepts in the DDA 1995 were, instead:

- "Less Favourable Treatment" for a reason related to a person's disability.

- Failure to make a "Reasonable Adjustment".

"Reasonable adjustment" is the radical concept that made the DDA so different. Instead of "indirect discrimination" where someone can take action if they have been disadvantaged by a policy or practice, reasonable adjustment is an active approach that requires employers, schools, and service providers to take steps to remove barriers from participation by people with disabilities. The concept is retained in the Equality Act.

The Equality Act 2010

In 2010, the Equality Act was introduced to codify the complicated and numerous array of Acts and Regulations, which formed the basis of anti-discrimination law in Great Britain. These were, primarily, the Equal Pay Act 1970, the Sex Discrimination Act 1975, the Race Relations Act 1976, the Disability Discrimination Act 1995 and three major statutory instruments protecting discrimination in employment on grounds of religion or belief, sexual orientation and age.

The Equality Act defines eight "Protected Characteristics" for people who use services. These are:

- Age
- Disability
- Gender reassignment
- Pregnancy and maternity
- Race
- Religion and belief
- Sex (gender)
- Sexual orientation

Additional resources

These documents can be found on the website www.inclusivechoice.com:

- *What equality law means for you as an education provider - schools*
- *Equality Act (2010) easy read*
- *Equality Act (2010) - What do I need to know - Disability quick start guide*
- *Equality Act (2010)*
- *Equality Act (2010) - Explanatory Notes*

DEFINITIONS OF DISABILITY AND SEN

Disability

In the Equality Act, "Disability" is defined as follows:

> *A person has a disability for the purposes of this Act if he has a physical or mental impairment which has a substantial and long-term adverse effect on his ability to carry out normal day-to-day activities.*

The test of whether impairment affects normal day-to-day activity is whether it affects one or more of the following: mobility; manual dexterity; physical co-ordination; continence; ability to lift, carry or otherwise move everyday objects; speech, hearing or eyesight; memory or ability to concentrate, learn or understand; or the perception of risk of physical danger.

The EA also covers people with:

- Severe disfigurements
- Impairments which are controlled or corrected by the use of medication, prostheses, or other aids (excluding spectacles)
- Progressive symptomatic conditions

- A history of impairment
- Cancer, HIV or multiple sclerosis at the point of diagnosis.

However, the EA does not cover addiction to or dependence on nicotine, tobacco or other non-prescribed drugs or substances; hay fever; or certain mental illnesses, which have anti-social consequences. Accordingly, it might be possible for a pupil to have special educational needs, but not be disabled for the purposes of the EA, and vice versa (although the majority of pupils with disabilities will also have some special educational needs).

Special Educational Needs (SEN)

Not all children who are defined as disabled will have SEN. For example, those with severe asthma, arthritis or diabetes may not have SEN but may have rights under the EA. Similarly, not all children with SEN will be defined as having a disability under the Equality Act. The Equality and Human Rights Commission's Code of Practice for schools is helpful in explaining this in more detail.

The Department for Children, Schools, and Families defines children with SEN as:

> *Having learning difficulties or disabilities, which make it harder for them to learn or access education than most other children of the same age.*

Children have a learning difficulty if they:

a. Have a significantly greater difficulty in learning than the majority of children of the same age; or

b. Have a disability which prevents or hinders them from making use of educational facilities of a kind generally provided for children of the same age in schools within the area of the local education authority

c. Are under compulsory school age and fall within the definition at (a) or (b) above or would so do if special educational provision was not made for them.

Children are not regarded as having a learning difficulty solely because they are not being taught in their first language.

Hidden impairments

Hidden impairments are those, which might not be immediately obvious. However, they are also covered under the definition of disability. Examples include:

- Attention Deficit Hyperactivity Disorder (ADHD)
- Dyslexia
- Autism
- Physical co-ordination
- Incontinence
- Ability to lift, carry or otherwise move everyday objects

- Speech, hearing or eyesight (unless correctable by spectacles)
- Memory or ability to concentrate, learn or understand;
- Perception of risk of physical danger

Additional resources

These booklets can be found at the Inclusive Choice website on the "Books" resource tab:

- *Duties and definitions*
- *SEN Code Of Practice*
- *Code Of Practice for schools*
- *Early years and the Disability Discrimination Act*
- *Including Me - Managing complex health needs in schools and early years settings*
- *Disability Discrimination Act 1995*

THE DISABILITY DISCRIMINATION DUTIES

The Equality Act makes it illegal to discriminate against a person with a disability for a reason related to their disability, or for a reason related to their disability. It also makes it illegal to have rules, policies, or practices which apply to everyone but which particularly disadvantages people with disabilities. Schools are required to make *Reasonable Adjustments* to allow children with disabilities to fully partake in the activities of your school.

These requirements can be encapsulated into the two duties inherited from the Disability Discrimination Act:

Less Favourable Treatment

Children with disabilities are entitled not to be treated less favourably than a child without a disability for a reason relating to their disability, without reasonable justification.

Reasonable Adjustments

Children with disabilities are entitled to have reasonable adjustments made with respect to admission arrangements or in the provision of education and associated services, to prevent them being placed at a substantial disadvantage, unless the refusal to make those adjustments can be justified.

Additional resources

These booklets can be found at the Inclusive Choice website on the "Books" resource tab:

- *Equality Act (2010) - What do I need to know - Disability quick start guide*
- *What equality law means for you as an education provider - schools*
- *Code of Practice for Services, Public Functions and Associations*
- *Duties and definitions*
- *Early years and the Disability Discrimination Act*

APPRECIATIVE INQUIRY

Appreciative Inquiry is an approach, which looks at issues in a different way. It asks us not to look for what is broken and fix it, but rather to look at what works. We approach our schools with an appreciative eye. It is not about looking at what we do through "rose tinted glasses" but about recognising our achievements.

Small actions lead to big results

For example, suppose you receive the results of a survey that was designed to assess parental satisfaction. It says that 94% of your school's children's parents are happy with the service that you provide. What would you normally do? You may decide to interview the 6% that are unhappy. Appreciative Inquiry says you should first ask the 94% what you did to make them happy.

It is easy to view this as a rather simplistic way to face your school's biggest challenges, but it is also easy to be cynical and dismissive of this approach. We should encourage a working environment of appreciation of what works, which will then lead to a positive shift in attitudes. At the end of your next meeting, try asking this simple question "What did we do well in this meeting"?

This method uses questions designed to encourage people to talk about their experiences of a particular issue. It aims to encourage participants to focus on finding solutions to issues and their experiences of 'what works'. It can be empowering, as it gives people the confidence to think broadly and take risks. It can help to build relationships and to improve understanding. It can also be useful in encouraging motivation, particularly if participants feel resistant to change or that they are being criticised.

For more about Appreciative Inquiry, have a look at Sue Annis Hammond's book "Thin Book of Appreciative Inquiry".

HUMAN RIGHTS: RIGHTS, RESPECT AND RESPONSIBILITIES

The right to be treated with dignity and respect and to feel safe in our environment is a fundamental right. New research by the EHRC, *"How fair is Britain?,2010"*, has found that bullying based on pupils' identities, whether it be homophobic, transphobic, race, disability-related or religiously motivated, remains a widespread problem and is limiting the achievements of those who are bullied.

At school, young people with disabilities and special educational needs are most at risk of being bullied, and two-thirds of lesbian, gay and transgender secondary school pupils report that they have been victims of often severe bullying (17% of those bullied reported having received death threats). The study found that nearly two in ten of all school pupils said that they do not feel physically safe at school.

UNICEF Rights Respecting School Award

A "Rights Respecting School" is one where all sections of the school community know about and value the UN Convention on the Rights of the Child and everyone uses the language of rights, respect and responsibility. The strong emphasis on the UN Convention on the Rights of the Child highlights the importance of respecting the rights of others and of personal and collective responsibility.

Promoting community cohesion in your school from a Rights Respecting standpoint can have a dramatic positive effect on achieving outcomes such as:

- More positive attitudes towards diversity in society and the reduction of prejudice;
- Overall school improvement including better learning and academic standards;
- Improved behaviour and relationships;
- Improved pupil self-esteem.

Equal rights, equal respect

Anne Hughes is the remarkable head-teacher who introduced a Rights Respecting framework At Knights Enham junior school, and subsequently became the first in the world to be awarded a UNICEF level 2 Rights Respecting School Award.

Based on an idea from Nova Scotia, Anne implemented this approach over two terms with one of the school's two Year 6 classes. She said "Very quickly we started to notice differences in behaviour and attitude between the two classes. The children who were taught about human rights were more tolerant of one another, they listened to each other, and they were more interested in global issues."

The change has been remarkable since the introduction of the rights-based approach. "The children are more confident; they are better behaved and happy to come to school." The school statistics show that since the school adopted the rights-based approach in 2003, unauthorised absence has dropped, exclusions are down, and SATS scores have doubled.

Anne now implements a human rights-based approach throughout the three schools she is responsible for and things have continued to improve. One school was struggling with poor behaviour and low SATs results and had a decline in numbers. She says "Since then it has had two good years of vastly improved results, behaviour has improved with only one fixed term exclusion last year and none so far this year and is now becoming a very popular school within the area".

Community cohesion

Your school now has a general duty to promote community cohesion. Ofsted are required to consider and report on your school's contribution to community cohesion.

Community cohesion refers to the aspect of togetherness and bonding exhibited by members of a community - the "glue" that holds a community together. This might include features such as a sense of common belonging or cultural similarity. It means working towards a society in which there is a common vision and sense of belonging by all members; a society in which the diversity of people's backgrounds and circumstances is appreciated and valued; a society in which similar life opportunities are available to all; and a society in which strong and positive relationships exist and continue to be developed in the workplace, in schools and in the wider community.

The curriculum for all maintained schools should promote the spiritual, moral, cultural, mental and physical development of pupils, and prepare pupils at your school for the opportunities, responsibilities and experiences of later life.

Community from a school's perspective

For schools, the term 'community' has a number of dimensions including:

- your school community – the pupils it serves, their families and your school's staff;
- the community within which your school is located – your school in its geographical community and the people who live or work in that area;
- the community of Britain - all schools are by definition part of this community;
- the global community – formed by EU and international links.

In addition, schools themselves create communities – for example, the networks formed by schools of the same or different faiths, or by schools that are part of the specialist schools network. The Rights Respecting framework described above is an excellent way to promote community cohesion.

Additional resources

- *"Right Here, Right Now"* is a a free resource for Key Stage 3 citizenship teachers. It aims to link the concept of universal human rights with everyday experiences

and helps teachers examine human rights issues such as identity and diversity with pupils as part of the new KS3 citizenship curriculum in secondary schools in England.
`www.bihr.org.uk/projects/teaching-resources`

- The Rights Respecting Schools Award (RRSA) recognises achievement in putting the United Nations Convention on the Rights of the Child (CRC) at the heart of a school's planning, policies, practice and ethos.
`www.unicef.org.uk/rrsa`

- *"We Are All Born To Be Free"*, Amnesty International, 2008.
Recommended for school libraries as it is suitable for all ages.

INTRODUCING THE EQUALITY DUTY

Remember to apply Appreciative Inquiry to all that you do when working towards your equality duty. You should encourage a working environment of appreciation of what already works in your school. It is important that you recognise your achievements in this area, as without this type of approach towards your work it will be easy to lose focus and become despondent. Most of us don't think about our day to day activities that much. We go to work, travel on buses, cook our meals, help our children with their homework, attend hospital appointments and visit the library. These aspects of our life are fully accessible.

Many indicators show that for people with disabilities life isn't like this. There remains considerable work to be done to get to this point. To start on the road to accomplish this, in 2005 the Disability Equality Duty (DED) legislation came into force as part 5A of the Disability Discrimination Act. This legislation has now been subsumed into the Equality Act, 2010. The Equality Duty is meant to ensure that all public bodies - such as central and local government, schools, health trusts and emergency services – pay 'due regard' to the promotion of equality for people with disabilities in every area of their work.

Previously there were three separate equality duties, disability, race, and gender. You may now wish to combine these three into a single one (a Single Equality Duty), or you may leave the three separate. Almost all the requirements of the 2005 Disability Equality Duty are still present in the new equality duty, although there have been some name changes.

The equality duty is in two parts - a General Duty and a Specific Duty. Both apply to all publicly funded schools, and responsibility for the duty lies with the governing body or the proprietor. The EHRC can take action against schools that have not met their duties. Academies and free schools are 'public authorities' for the purposes of the Equality Act. That means they are bound by the public sector equality duty (PSED).

In simple terms, whenever your school make decisions, which might impact differently on girls, on members of particular ethnic groups, on members of particular religious groups, or on people with disabilities, they must give particular consideration to the issues which arise, and try to reduce any adverse impact.

The duties require schools to take steps not just to eliminate unlawful discrimination and harassment, but also to actively promote equality. This is very similar to what your school should already be doing under the previous Disability Equality Duty.

The General Duty

The general duty requires schools, when carrying out their functions, to have due regard to the need to:

- Eliminate discrimination, harassment and victimisation.
- Advance equality of opportunity between people with disabilities and people without disabilities.
- Foster good relations between people with disabilities and people without disabilities.

These are called the *three aims* of the Equality Duty. They replace the six elements of the 2005 Disability Equality Duty. However, in practice very little has changed, because the old six elements are all included in the new three aims:

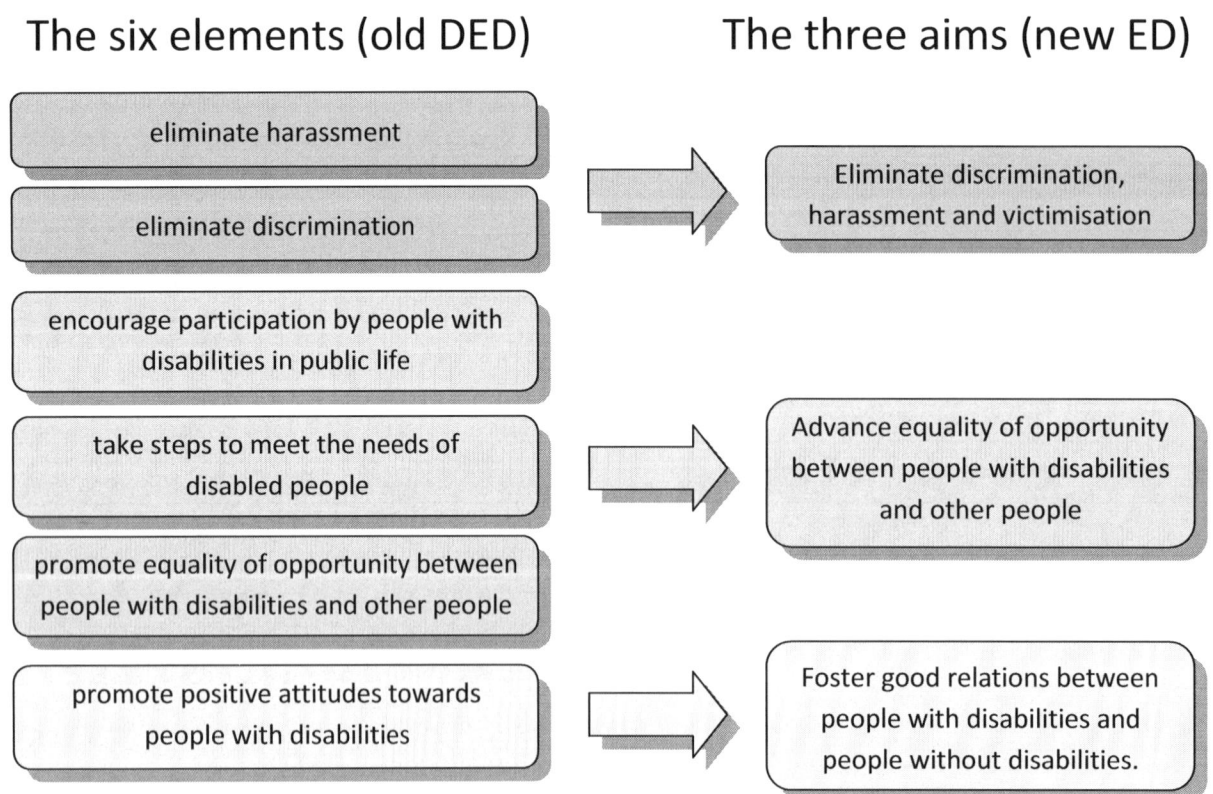

The six elements (old DED)

eliminate harassment

eliminate discrimination

encourage participation by people with disabilities in public life

take steps to meet the needs of disabled people

promote equality of opportunity between people with disabilities and other people

promote positive attitudes towards people with disabilities

The three aims (new ED)

Eliminate discrimination, harassment and victimisation

Advance equality of opportunity between people with disabilities and other people

Foster good relations between people with disabilities and people without disabilities.

The three aims apply across schools' duties to pupils with disabilities, staff and parent/carers with disabilities, and other users of your school. It does not bring in new rights for people with disabilities, but it does require schools to take a more proactive approach to promoting disability equality and eliminating discrimination.

The specific duty

The specific duty requires your school to demonstrate how you are meeting the general duty. In effect, the general duty sets out *what* you have to do and the specific duty sets out *how* you have to do it, and what you need to record as evidence of what you have done.

You are required to undertake the development of your equality duty documents in a particular way and to include particular elements. You must engage with pupils with disabilities and parents in the preparation of these documents, they should not just be a description of what you and your school want to do. Only children with disabilities and parents (and to a certain extent staff) who use your school know what really matters to them. You must describe in your documents how you have engaged with people with disabilities and involved them.

In addition, your equality scheme must set out your arrangements for obtaining Equality Information on the effect your school's policies have on:

- the educational opportunities available to and the achievements of pupils with disabilities;
- your methods for assessing the impact of your current or proposed policies and practices on disability equality;
- the steps you are going to take to meet the general duty (your school's action plan);
- the arrangements for using information to support the review of the action plan in the future.

The 2005 Disability Equality Duty had three *Specific Duties*. These have been renamed in the Equality Act:

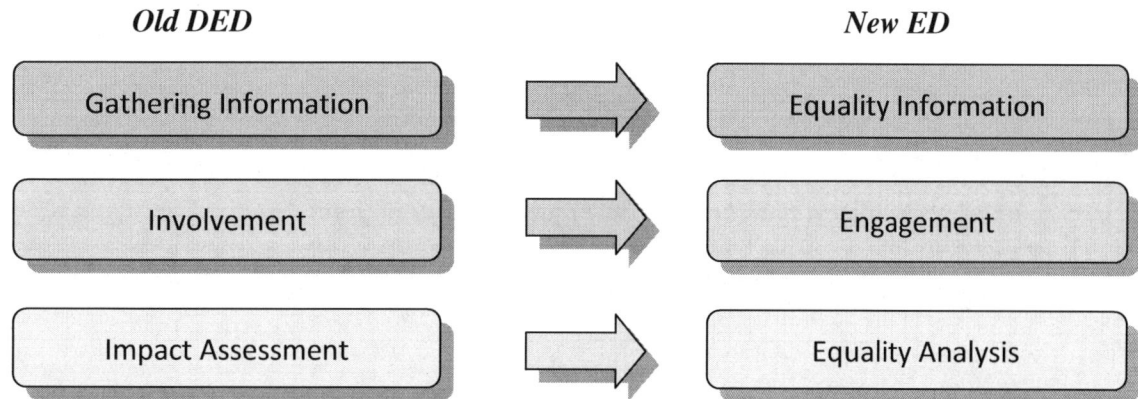

In addition, the requirements to regularly review your scheme and make action plans to improve have been termed *"Equality Objectives"*. After you have set your equality objectives, you will be expected to publish information that enables both you and the public to measure how successful you have been in meeting them. You would be expected to do this at least annually.

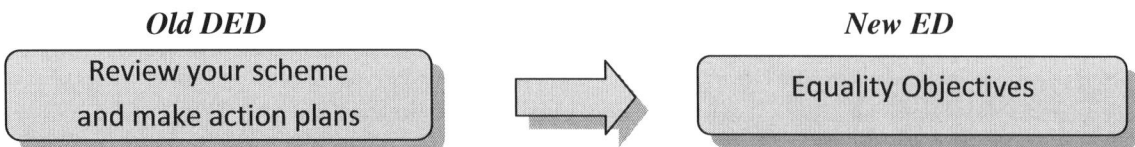

Old DED → *New ED*

Review your scheme and make action plans → Equality Objectives

The Race Equality Duty has the same three aims as the Disability Equality Duty. However, the Gender Equality Duty differs slightly in that there are two aims you need to pay due regard to when carrying out all school functions:

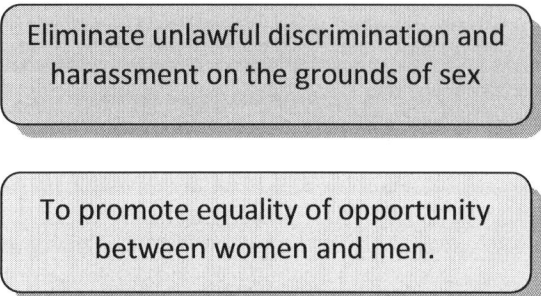

Eliminate unlawful discrimination and harassment on the grounds of sex

To promote equality of opportunity between women and men.

Although this is slightly different to the Race and Disability duty the overall ethos of the PSED in regard to school's equality duties is the same and I have reflected this in the single equality scheme example (see appendix 9).

Relevance

The General Equality Duty applies to public bodies, whatever their size. The way in which it is implemented, however, should be appropriate to the size and the nature of its functions. For a school, this means everything that you are *required* to do as well as everything that you are allowed to do. Teaching of pupils is obviously the primary service, but the duty also covers policies and procedures, budgetary decisions, allocating resources, regulation, and employment of staff, audits and inspections, external communication, commissioning services, procuring goods, partnerships, management of premises, etc.

For a school, certain protected characteristics will obviously be more relevant than others, and certain functions of your school are more relevant than others. This should be reflected in the work that you do and the information that you publish.

What needs to be published?

What needs to be in your equality scheme? You may wish to present your objectives within a similar document to your old DES if that has been an effective approach for organising your equality information and for communicating your plans to stakeholders.

Your existing DES can become the basis of your new published information. You must meet all the other publication requirements, which are detailed below.

Compliance with the General Equality Duty

You must publish sufficient information to demonstrate your compliance with the General Equality Duty (the three aims), and this must be updated at least annually thereafter.

This must include:

- The effect of your policies and practices on children with protected characteristics in accordance with the three aims.
- The analysis you have undertaken to establish whether the policies and practices have furthered the three aims.
- Details of the information you considered in carrying out this analysis.
- Details of the engagement you undertook.

Equality Objectives

You must publish your equality objectives by 5th April 2012, and every four years after that. This should include:

- Objectives you intend to achieve to meet one or more aims of the general equality duty.
- Details of the engagement that you undertook in developing these objectives.

The objectives should be specific and measurable and should set out how progress will be measured.

The Equality and Human Rights Commission would normally expect to see the information published broken down by protected group. It would usually include:

- Performance information, for example pupil attainment.
- Access to services (lessons, school trips, etc and reasonable adjustments put in place).
- Satisfaction with services
- Complaints from parents, with an indication of reasons for complaints.

Managing the Process in School

You will find it helpful to appoint a working group of three or four people to steer the development of your school's equality scheme and to report to the governing body. They should meet regularly to ensure the process continues, and is not forgotten about until the day before the review or Ofsted inspection is due! Ideally, the working group would consist of at least a senior manager and a person with a disability:

A senior manager

The scope of the Equality Duty is across your school's responsibilities, so at least one member of the group needs to be a senior manager, in order to draw on links with every area of your school's work, and to have the authority necessary to implement policies. The SENCO should not be expected to lead the process.

A person with a disability

It is required to have a representative with a disability within the group, since when you come to draw up your plan you will have to state how people with disabilities have been involved. This person can be a member of staff, a parent, or a senior pupil.

Other members

It may be helpful to incorporate a range of perspectives into the group by recruiting across curriculum and pastoral responsibilities, across length of service in your school, across teaching and non-teaching responsibilities. The SENCO might be included because many of the pupils with SEN will also count as being disabled and the SENCO will know them well. However, not all pupils with disabilities have SEN and it should not be assumed that the SENCO has sole responsibility for the EA duties: they are as much the responsibility of the key stage co-ordinator, or the head of Maths, as they are of the SENCO!

Incorporating your accessibility plan

Schools should already be providing for the additional needs of pupils with disabilities and special educational needs, through the EA and SENDA.

The planning requirements from the Equality Act require that schools develop accessibility strategies and plans to improve access to school education for pupils with disabilities, by:

- increasing access to the curriculum for pupils with disabilities;
- making improvements to the physical environment of your school to increase access to education and associated services;
- making written information accessible in a range of different ways for pupils with disabilities, where it is provided in writing for pupils who are not disabled.

If your school is already complying with your duties under the EA (making Reasonable Adjustments, and avoiding discrimination), and has a well-developed accessibility plan, you may find that you are well on the way to meeting the DED already.

Do I still have to publish an equality scheme?

Under the specific duties, there is no legal requirement to produce or publish a formal 'equality scheme' as there was previously. However, if you feel this is an effective format to publish your objectives (and how you will measure progress) and your equality information, then you can choose to develop a 'scheme'. How you set out your information is not as important as the quality of the information, and how this was acquired and analysed. You should present the information in a manner that is reasonably accessible to the public, as an individual document or as part of another document.

You should also remember that producing an equality scheme alone will not fulfil your obligations under the general equality duty - eliminating discrimination, harassment and victimisation, advancing equality of opportunity, and fostering good relations between people with disabilities and people without disabilities. Actions and achievements are much more important than words and documents.

It would be good practice to publish your objectives and the progress you have made towards them in your annual report. Putting regular updates on your website shows pupils, parents, and inspectors your good intentions and how you are realising them. It also acts as encouragement for future participation for those that have an interest in the DED.

Publication

The documents must be in writing, and must be published. It can be published as a separate document or you may wish to combine it into a single one (a Single Equality Duty), which would combine your other equality duties.

Wherever it is published, you must be able to provide a copy to anyone asking for it and the elements of the duty need to be easily identifiable. Ask yourself, "How readily can parents or visitors get hold of a copy of the document?"

POLICY AND PRACTICE

When reviewing your policies and practices you need to have due regard to the need to advance equality. Your school policies and practices must reflect this due regard in all that you do.

Ofsted inspectors can only make judgements based on what they are presented with. If a school is judged to be no better than 'satisfactory' in relation to equality and diversity then its overall effectiveness is unlikely to be better than 'good', and likely in fact to be similarly no better than satisfactory. It is for that reason that you have to find a cohesive tie between your policy and practice because without this cohesion you will have made it unnecessarily difficult to show how your school is achieving in it PSED.

New areas like sexual orientation, gender reassignment and maternity and pregnancy may need new approaches and a new line of thinking for you. Remember your own attitude may be what is really holding your school back to becoming outstanding and remarkable.

Here are some questions you may wish to consider when producing or reviewing your policies, but this is not an exhaustive list:

- Does the policy affect pupils, staff or the wider community, and therefore potentially have a significant effect in terms of equality? Remember that relevance of a policy will depend not only on the number of those affected but also by the significance of the effect on them.
- Does the policy relate to things that the engagement process has identified as being important to people?
- Does the policy affect different protected groups differently?
- Does the policy relate to an area with known inequalities (for example, people with disabilities, racist or homophobic bullying in schools).

If you decide that a policy is not relevant to equality, you should document this, along with the reasons which brought you to this decision. A simple statement of no relevance to equality without any supporting information is not sufficient, nor is a statement that no information is available.

Collecting your information and using it.

Identifying your strengths and weaknesses will be important in order to produce non-discriminatory policies and relevant, meaningful schemes and action plans. If you feel your school is effective in identifying priorities for action and you believe your school has certain strengths in a particular area then you need to ask yourself:

- How did you do the equality analysis for this?
- How can I show the evidence for this?

When looking for equality evidence you must try to be objective and look to others for support. Your school should be looking to engage with more people with protected characteristics. Engagement is the only way to ensure you get a realistic and non-biased view of how your school really is meeting its duty. What can your local authority do to support you? They may be able to facilitate engagement with different groups using their connections and knowledge with voluntary sector groups and through government training programmes.

Schools with policies and action plans with set targets for the duties are more likely to develop positive practice and achieve improvements to pupil outcomes.

OUTCOME BASED ACCOUNTABILITY

Outcome Based Accountability (OBA) is an approach that is recognized and used by the Department for Education. The OBA model offers tools and a coherent framework for strategic planning; evidence based commissioning and monitoring what works to improve outcomes.

OBA is a disciplined way of thinking and taking action that can be used to improve the quality of life in communities, and improve the performance of services and agencies.

Outputs are defined as achievements for your school, for example, recording extra attendance data for children with disabilities or alterations to the building. However, outcomes are achievements, which lead to children with disabilities and families being better off.

OBA makes a careful distinction between *outcomes* and *outputs*. This is important because measuring success on the basis of outputs alone can be misleading. It is entirely possible for schools to deliver services that meet a wide range of outputs or process targets, including timeliness, staff recruitment and participation levels, yet still not succeed in improving *outcomes* for children with disabilities and their families.

In terms of the DED…

- The *outcomes* are the three aims of the general duty for children with disabilities, parents, staff and communities (see page 49).
- *Equality Analysis* is the measure which helps quantify the achievement of an outcome. For example, promoting positive attitudes, or eliminating discrimination (see page 49).
- *Performance Measure* is how well a program, agency or service is working. We ask ourselves:
    - How much did we do?
    - How well did we do it?
    - Is anyone better off?

    The question *"Is anyone better off?"* refers to outcomes for children with disabilities and their families.

More details can be found in the book *"Trying Hard Is Not Good Enough"* by Mark Friedman, the creator of OBA.

2   SECTIONS OF THE SCHEME

ENGAGEMENT

"Engagement" is another way of saying "involving and interacting with your pupils, staff and parents with disabilities", asking them what is most important to them, what are their greatest concerns about how your school provides for people with disabilities.

Engagement in the context of the equality duty covers a range of different activities, from formal public consultations to direct engagement with people with disabilities, in designing and delivering better services, and improving the educational achievements of SEN and pupils with disabilities.

Engagement can tell you where you are successful in promoting equality and where action is still needed. It is particularly useful where there are information gaps. Engagement can help you to fill these gaps, and it can give you an idea of how accurate your information is. This means whether or not there are any differences between how you think you are performing, and the experiences of people with disabilities.

Stop, think, listen - engage

You may think that you don't have any children with disabilities, parents, or staff. However, many people are unaware just how many people are classed as disabled. Refer back to the section on hidden impairments on page 12. Can you say for sure that you don't have any pupils with a hidden impairment? Look at the table on page 97. This allows you to work out the expected number of pupils you will have with a variety of common disabilities.

The Disability Equality Duty requires you to find out about these people. This is described in the section on Equality Analysis (page 49).

After gathering all the information you can, if you still find there are very few pupils with disabilities in your school, it may be beneficial to cluster together with other small schools to form a consultative group. In this way a lot of the work involved in the duty can be shared.

Pupils with disabilities, staff and parents should be involved in all stages of the development of the scheme: in identifying the priorities, how these priorities should be met in the action plans, and how your school should assess its progress.

The engagement must be real. If engagement is done well, it can help to improve the design and delivery of services, and the policies and practices affecting your pupils. It can help increase trust in your school. It can lead to efficiency gains by improving service design at the planning stages. You should listen to the views of pupils with disabilities, staff and parents and carers, and develop your plan in response to what you hear, not what you would *like* to hear.

However, getting the engagement right is not straightforward and it is likely that your first plan will be developed in the light of the views that you can hear more readily. Part of the action plan will then need to focus on developing the engagement of pupils with disabilities, staff and parents over a period of time. This way you will learn what works and the engagement of pupils with disabilities, staff and parents should improve and deepen over time.

Ensure that all staff who are tasked with involving disability organisations and people with disabilities receive Disability Equality training, because it's difficult to 'do the duty' without knowing exactly what the law requires.

Engagement may also help you avoid costly changes to services or buildings at a later stage, as well as avoiding tribunals. It can also help to identify whether *more* favourable treatment (called *positive action*, see page 66) is necessary in order to meet particular needs. Schools that meet the needs of people with disabilities better are likely to be more effective in the longer term when it comes to:

- How to achieve 'good' or better Ofsted judgements
- Positive and measurable outcomes for SEN and children with disabilities
- Better relationships with parents

Engaging with pupils with disabilities

Small schools may have trouble finding enough pupils with disabilities to achieve successful engagement. In addition to children with disabilities currently on role at your school, you may also like to include:

- Pupils with disabilities who have left your school.
- Those who may be coming to your school, for example from feeder primary schools.
- Pupils leaving your school. Exit interviews with pupils with disabilities leaving your school each year may provide useful insights. Often people find it easier to be completely frank when they are leaving an organisation.

It is helpful if the parents of pupils with disabilities disclose their children's disabilities to you. This must be handled sensitively of course. Disclosure is covered in more detail on page 79.

Other ideas for engaging with pupils with disabilities are through your school council, by meeting with small groups of pupils, by creating a more informal social occasion for pupils with disabilities, through an e-forum, or by arranging a meeting across the local authority or a cluster of schools. You can adapt your approach to accommodate pupils' preferences.

Example

Many pupils with an Autistic Spectrum Disorder (ASD) find forms of consultation like questionnaires, e-forums or online discussion rooms easier than face-to-face communication or meetings. Student councils also represent a constructive method for pupils to be involved with your schools development, and you should consider how accessible they are to people with an ASD and how their views are represented on the council.

Example

A school decides to seek feedback on its bullying policy from pupils with an ASD on its school council. However, this reveals that there are no pupils with an ASD (or indeed any pupils with disabilities) on the council.

This prompts your school to consider the lack of representation and investigate whether the student council is accessible for pupils with an ASD. However, your school is not able to identify any pupils with an ASD. It decides to investigate whether this is simply statistical - that is, your school is so small that the lack of pupils with an ASD is simply due to chance (see Appendix on page 97 for a table showing the likelihood of this) - or whether potential pupils are actively avoiding your school. Your school engages with the local community by contacting local autistic groups through `www.info.autism.org.uk`, and contacts neighbouring schools and the local authority to help it understand its position.

Example

A school sets up an open meeting for pupils with disabilities to gather their views for producing their Equality scheme. They notice that pupils with communication difficulties find it hard to join in. Some don't take part; some talk for long periods without recognising others' contributions.

Your school decides to ask the pupils how best to support them. Some said they would like support during the meeting to help them join in. Some say they would like to contribute using an email group instead.

Example

A school is refurbishing its décor in part of your school. In order to involve all the pupils and parents in the process, a questionnaire is sent to all pupils. This allows children with disabilities and their parents to give their views on any sensory problems that may arise during and after the refurbishment.

As a result, softer more calming colours - which lower sensory arousal levels for pupils with certain disabilities - are used to paint the classrooms and hallways. Your school bells are disconnected during the changes and this has a positive effect on one child's behaviour during and after the lunch break as the bell had a very shrill ring that affected the child's oversensitive hearing. Through consultation with the pupil and parents, a new bell with a less severe sound is installed.

Example class exercise

What children with disabilities like and don't like about their school

This exercise can involve children with and without disabilities and adults in determining the areas of your school that children with disabilities like, and the areas they find difficult or unpleasant. The idea is to create a large poster showing "hot spots" and "grot spots".

The required materials are:

- paper
- coloured markers
- coloured stickers

Depending on their age and disability, some pupils may find drawing the map difficult so you may like to draw the maps in advance.

The result of the exercise should be presented to the next school council, and recommendations made to improve the areas that were deemed unpleasant or difficult.

Class exercise

Identifying Barriers for People with disabilities

A good starting point for training on Disability Equality is to identify all the barriers in the environment, attitude and how things are organised in your school.

Each Group takes a different disability subject and tries to work on what barriers might exist for someone who has this disability, and what solutions there may be. If you have any pupils with any of these disabilities, you may choose not to use that disability, or you may ask the pupil if they would wish to contribute. This exercise is not solely to concentrate on disability but also to explore what can make life difficult for people when they are treated in a discriminatory way, and may include difference in skin colour, religion or language. Explore ways in which the children can think about attitude, behaviour and beliefs (refer back to RRS page).

What barriers does your school pose for pupils who...

- Are blind or have a visual impairment
- Have Tourette's syndrome
- Are deaf or have a hearing impairment
- Have a mobility impairment and/or use a wheelchair
- Have a significant learning difficulty
- Have been labelled as autistic,
- Have hidden impairments including speech and language, sickle cell, epilepsy or diabetes or HIV?
- Have mental health issues.

Remember it will be virtually impossible to have any type of meaningful engagement with people with disabilities if your school is weak in its understanding of the Equality Act in particular the *Reasonable Adjustments* duty. These are described in my previous book "The Equality Act for Educational Professionals".

Example

> Staff consulted a pupil with a physical disability pupil, Carmel, and her mother about how the school could support her in getting the most out of an

adventure holiday. This ensured a really positive experience that enhanced Carmel's confidence.

After progressing to secondary school, Carmel was invited back to her primary school to comment on access for children with disabilities and adults. This resulted in many changes around the school, from car parking arrangements to the design of the waste bin in the toilet for people with disabilities. Carmel is now on long-term work experience at the school and is involved in all aspects of classroom support.

As well as helping to design the new accessible outdoor activity trail, Carmel is also beginning to support a vulnerable pupil with a disability and his concerned parent to maximise the opportunities available to children with disabilities at the school. Having Carmel regularly involved with the school over many years has enriched and deepened staff understanding of disability. It has also increased pupils' learning about disability, as well as providing a role model for other pupils with disabilities.

Engagement of staff with disabilities

You should involve employees with disabilities working at your school. If there aren't any you could engage with those working at other local schools, or for the local authority. This may be done through a local teacher union network, an e-forum, or meetings across a cluster of schools. Offer exit interviews to all staff who leave, disabled and non-disabled. Such interviews might provide useful information for your school's scheme and might also offer some insight into factors affecting disclosure.

School management should create a staff culture that is welcoming of difference. This can be done by giving time off school day for colleagues with disabilities to meet together in a forum. Workplace trade unions may also have much to offer. Any forums set up should include other groups of staff - it is important to brief all staff about the DED and how management are planning to consult, to allay fears and misconceptions. Some issues most commonly identified by staff with disabilities are:

- Reasonable adjustments in terms of timetable, and location of teaching rooms
- Overcoming barriers to short-listing for promoted posts
- Access to ongoing professional development
- Extra time off arising from their impairment not counting on sickness monitoring
- Not wanting to be used for break and other ancillary duties
- Provision of light duties and flexible working to take account of fatigue
- Being consulted

Example

A staff questionnaire reveals only one member of staff with a disability. Aware that staff may be reluctant to disclose a disability, the school decides to...

- promote awareness of the Equality Act and the legal protection that it offers staff who are covered by it
- explain that disclosure can enable the school to make reasonable adjustments
- raise awareness of the local authority policy on harassment and bullying
- promote awareness of the support available to members of staff with disabilities.

The school also decides they should examine their recruitment process with a view to encouraging applicants with disabilities. They decide to...

- offer an interview to all applicants with disabilities for a job at the school, if they meet the minimum criteria;
- investigate the employers' 'two ticks' scheme
- contact local teacher training schools to offer to be a placement for trainee teachers with disabilities.

Example

A secondary school sets up a working group to advise on the school's disability equality scheme. The group is aware of evidence that teachers with disabilities, and particularly those with mental health conditions such as depression, may be reluctant to disclose a disability. The working party only knows of one member of staff with a disability, who has cancer, and they ask her:

- if she would join the working group;
- what the school needs to do to enable more staff to feel comfortable about disclosing a disability; and
- how they might then involve staff with disabilities in the development of the school's scheme.

The member of staff does not want to join the working group, but is happy to make some points for the working group to consider. She also suggests that within the school cluster (six schools) a small group of staff with disabilities might be formed to contribute to the development of schemes in the cluster schools.

Arising from this discussion, the working group agrees the following actions:

- the school will seek general advice from a local support group about disability friendly policies;
- a teacher on the working group will consult his union about the support available to teachers with disabilities
- the school will explore, with its partner schools, the possibility of setting up a cross-cluster group of staff with disabilities, with a view to involving them in considering what the schools in the cluster need to do to encourage staff to disclose a disability. Setting up this staff group is given high priority, so that the development and implementation of the scheme can be informed by the group.

Checklist for engagement with staff with disabilities

The following checklist can be useful when considering how you will involve staff with disabilities.

- ☐ Have you informed all staff about the Disability Equality Duty?

- ☐ Have you initiated any disability equality training for staff?

- ☐ Have you got different engagement mechanisms in place such as online forums, or groups for staff with disabilities?

- ☐ Have you ensured that you are actually involving staff with disabilities and not just consulting with them (for example, a questionnaire to all staff is a method of consultation)?

- ☐ Are your engagement mechanisms effective? Are they proportionate, influential and transparent?

- ☐ Have you informed staff with disabilities why you want them to be involved?

- ☐ Have you ensured that you have included those with hidden disabilities?

- ☐ How have you involved part time staff, staff that work remotely, teaching and support staff?

The disability symbol ('Two Ticks')

Employers who show they have a positive attitude towards job applications from people with disabilities may show the Two Ticks logo on their job advertisements and other paperwork.

If an employer uses this symbol, it means they are positive about employing people with disabilities and will be keen to know about the abilities of the applicant. The symbol is awarded by Jobcentre Plus to employers in England, Scotland and Wales who have made commitments to employ, keep and develop the abilities of staff with disabilities.

Employers who use the disability symbol make five commitments regarding recruitment, training, retention, consultation and disability awareness:

1. to interview all applicants with disabilities who meet the minimum criteria for a job vacancy and to consider them on their abilities
2. to discuss with employees with disabilities, at any time but at least once a year, what both parties can do to make sure employees with disabilities can develop and use their abilities
3. to make every effort when employees become disabled to make sure they stay in employment
4. to take action to ensure that all employees develop the appropriate level of disability awareness needed to make these commitments work
5. to review these commitments each year and assess what has been achieved, plan ways to improve on them and let employees and Jobcentre Plus know about progress and future plans.

Is your school interested in getting the "Two Ticks"?

Staff disclosure

Staff with disabilities may be reluctant to declare their disability for fear of discrimination, which could impair their career prospects. However, self-declaration is necessary if schools are to record the number of staff with disabilities they employ accurately. The information is also important to guarantee equality for staff with disabilities.

Increasing the disclosure rate in school allows school management to tackle issues around disability discrimination and the concerns that staff have. There is no requirement to disclose a disability. Schools should create a workplace atmosphere that allows it to be safer for workers with disabilities to declare their disability status and the concerns that staff have.

The following checklist can be used to improve staff disclosure...

☐ Have staff been educated about disability and what is considered a disability?

☐ Have staff been informed why your school are asking staff to disclose?

☐ Are staff given different opportunities to disclose?

☐ Is the appropriate language being used in any questionnaires etc.?

☐ Are staff seeing a positive impact after disclosing?

An example questionnaire for staff with disabilities is shown below.

Question 1

Is there anything that your school could be doing to make it easier for staff to disclose a disability?

Question 2

What do you think that your school should change to improve the experience of its staff with disabilities? Your answer will help us to prioritise the actions we need to take.

Question 3

What barriers do you experience in your workplace that prevent you carrying out your job or hinder you carrying out your job?

Question 4

What do you think that your school is doing well to support the needs of its staff with disabilities?

Question 5

From your experience and/or observations, how well do you feel that the following support the needs of staff with disabilities:

Person	Very un-supportive	Un-supportive	Neutral	Supportive	Very supportive
Heads of Department					
Work colleagues					
Head teacher					
Other staff					

Question 6

How good do you think your school is doing in the following areas in relation to the inclusion of staff with disabilities:

Area	Very poor	Poor	Adequate	Good	Very good
Job application & interview process					
New staff induction					
Staff development					
Adjustments made for staff with disabilities					
Personal workspace (PC, desk etc)					
Disabled parking					
Annual Review process					
Access to advice and support in relation to disability issues					
Other (please give details)					

Question 7

Has this questionnaire missed any important issues or topics that affect the experience and participation of staff with disabilities at school. If so, what are they?

Thank you for your time and your contribution.

If you would like to be more involved in the development of your school's Disability Equality Scheme (for example, as a reader of the draft document or by contributing to later reviews of the Scheme), please provide your contact details below and we will be in touch with you.

Guidance on writing effective questionnaires can be found in Appendix 7.

Engagement with parents and carers with disabilities

It is well established that children do better at school when their parents are involved in their education, and supporting parents' participation is a central objective of education policy throughout the United Kingdom.

The DED requires you, when drawing up your equality scheme, to engage with parents. The legislation applies to all parents, and although it makes no specific reference to parents with disabilities, it has to be implemented in accordance with both the Specific and General Duties.

You must identify in your plan how you will not only reach out and positively encourage parents into your school, but also what mechanisms you will use to identify those parents with disabilities that might otherwise not access your school.

Involving parents with disabilities can go a lot further than just providing them with information. Your school should think about the following points when considering how best to improve engagement:

- How are elections for the governing body made fully accessible to all parents?
- Do you ensure that information, events and meetings are accessible to all parents?
- How do you promote a school ethos that values diversity, including children with disabilities and adults?
- Have you carried out access audits of all your school buildings?
- Do you seek advice from relevant organisations about how to make your buildings accessible?
- Do staff receive disability equality training?
- Do you welcome all parents into your school?

You may wish to involve governors, other family members, parents, children, members of the parent-teacher association, and volunteers with disabilities at your school, or members of the wider community such as local disability groups or individuals with disabilities using your school beyond your school day. Schools might arrange a meeting through the parent-teacher association or a local disability group, a meeting for their own school or for a cluster of schools.

Getting information to parents in 'easy-read' and other formats may be the first task. You may call meetings, possibly through the Parent Teacher Association, and set up a parent's forum for people with disabilities. Some parents with disabilities may not wish to be identified so it is important that your school projects a culture that is positive about disability, without being patronising. An example parent disclosure letter is in the appendix on page 80. The Parents with disabilities Network (www.disabledparentsnetwork.org.uk) may also be useful. Parents with disabilities should be especially encouraged to join the governing body.

Parents with disabilities are more likely to tell schools about their impairment if they believe it will lead to support that will benefit their child's education. The following tips will be helpful:

- All home-school communications to parents should be in formats that are accessible to them individually, and all staff involved with a parent with a disability should be aware of their communication support needs.

- If you present an informal, flexible and accessible atmosphere, it will facilitate engagement with parents with disabilities. Parents with learning disabilities and those experiencing mental distress particularly welcome oral communication and a personal contact at your school.
- Parents with disabilities of children with additional support needs often find formal meetings about their children's education very stressful. Schools can minimise this pressure by keeping meetings as informal as possible, providing parents with adequate information in accessible formats and being flexible about meeting times.
- While parents with disabilities benefit from anticipatory adjustments, their individual circumstances differ. You can provide the right initial support by communicating with the individual parent and can then plan how to anticipate and address future barriers.
- Disability awareness training for schools, including input for pupils, was identified as the best way of overcoming attitudinal barriers experienced by people with disabilities, particularly those with mental distress.
- Having staff with specific responsibility for parental engagement enhances parents with disabilities' involvement.

Issues most commonly identified by parents with disabilities are:

- Being supported to take their children to and from school
- Being able to access school information and newsletters
- Being able to access parents evenings and other school meetings
- Having access to Governor and PTA minutes in accessible formats
- Accessing school plays and shows
- Parking
- Promoting disability equality
- Access to facilities on the site

Example

A school is considering how to improve its communication with parents. Although it has previously tried to identify a group of parents with disabilities to get feedback from, this has only produced a very limited response. The school decides to ask a local organisation of parents with disabilities whether the organisation could give it some feedback. The local organisation agrees to this but suggests a meeting with a range of local schools so that they can have a wide-ranging discussion on communicating with parents with disabilities.

Example

As part of its continued communication with parents, a primary school sends a newsletter to all parents about the duty to promote disability equality. The newsletter highlights the school's responsibilities towards parents with disabilities as well as pupils with disabilities in the school. A definition of disability is also given so that parents who may not immediately identify themselves as being disabled see the broad coverage of the definition. The newsletter states that the school would be very interested to hear parents with disabilities' views on any school matter. Parents with disabilities who want to give information are asked to contact the deputy head to arrange an informal discussion

A range of views

Your scheme will be better informed if you hear the views of a diverse group of people with disabilities, but it is unlikely that an individual school will hear the voice of representatives of all impairment groups. Even within an impairment group, needs vary. For example, two people with a visual impairment may have widely differing needs; the needs of older people may differ from those of younger people. For this reason you should try to involve people with disabilities who have a perspective that goes wider than the effects of their own impairment and who bring with them an understanding of the barriers that exist for groups of pupils with disabilities, staff and parents.

Some tips for successful engagement

- Take an approach that is proportionate to your size and resources, and to the relevance of the issue to equality when deciding who to engage with and what methods to use.
- Establish what up-to-date information is already available and find out where your information gaps are before you plan your engagement. Look at local and national research, monitoring data and past consultations.
- Engagement only delivers benefits when it is done well so it should be clearly structured. Be clear about what you hope to achieve and about where you have scope to make any changes.
- Engagement can only be successful if it is adequately resourced and if it is accessible to enable a wide range of people to participate. Take steps to respect confidentiality and provide a safe environment.
- Successful engagement is influential and transparent. This requires reporting on the results of engagement, including an explanation of why certain points have not been taken on board. Good engagement produces tangible results for the authority and for participants.

- Consider undertaking joint engagement with other schools/authorities in the same geographical or service area. This can save resources and prevent stakeholders from becoming overstretched. It can encourage a more joined-up approach to equality.
- Build long-term relationships of trust with equality or voluntary sector organisations, or trade unions. This may involve formalising links with particular organisations or setting up a representative forum.
- Be mindful of diversity within protected groups and of the multiple barriers that many people face. Don't limit your engagement to only meeting with representative bodies.

Example

A visually impaired parent wishes to support their child in reading. How can the school help?

The school contacted the local authority's Visually Impairment Team, who provided them with a complete set of the books in large print format, and also provided further support and advice. The VI team also visited the school to raise awareness amongst the entire school staff.

Clear Vision (www.clearvisionproject.org) produce many books, including the Oxford Reading Tree, with Braille overlay, designed for children, but also useful for visually impaired parents.

http://www.disabledparentsnetwork.org.uk/cgibin/site/site.cgi?page=site/case_studies

Additional resources

These booklets can be found at the Inclusive Choice website on the "Books" resource tab:

- *Disability disclosure, confidentiality, and evidence in a Higher Education context - Extended Guidance Notes*
- *Disable parents involvement in their children's education – an examination of good practice*
- *Do you have a disability – yes or no*
- *Doing the duty overview*
- *Extending Inclusion*
- *Improving access for pupils with disabilities - School plans*
- *Inclusion of children with disabilities in primary school playgrounds*
- *Involving people with disabilities*
- *Making reasonable adjustments for disabled teachers (NUT)*
- *Meeting the needs of teachers with disabilities (NUT)*
- *Parental Confidence*

- *Parents with disabilities and schools - barriers to parental involvement in children's education*
- *Principles of good practice in involvement*
- *Promoting Disability Equality in Schools*
- *Supporting parents with disabilities*
- *Supporting parents with disabilities' involvement in their children's education*
- *Tool bag for supporting disabled teachers*

Equality information

Collection of information is necessary to support you in making decisions about what would most improve outcomes for people with disabilities. The information needs to be detailed enough to enable you to measure how well you are doing, and to assess the impact of the changes you make.

The collection of all your information may take some time, and can itself be an item on an action plan. Don't delay enacting any plans until better information has been collected though. Start with information that can be gathered easily, then improve your information gathering and analysis as part of the action plan.

Data remains central to the new inspection process. The challenge for your school will be to investigate the clues that your data gives about effectiveness and if the data reveal any underlining stories or weaknesses behind the figures.

The challenge is to obtain adequate information on each of the performance indicators for each protected characteristic (disability, race, etc). This can easily become a major undertaking, so be prudent and realistic in the number of indicators chosen. Each indicator will need data collection, analysis, and reporting systems behind it. Decide how to obtain the data you need to produce a meaningful, outcome based equality scheme. Think about:

1. What are the data collection methods?
2. Who will collect the data?
3. How often will the data be collected?
4. What is the cost and difficulty to collect the data?
5. Who will analyse the data?
6. Who will report the data?
7. Who will use the data?

Use existing information whenever possible. Look at what relevant information you already have that demonstrates how you are complying with the general equality duty.

What you need to show

Your plan must show how you are going to measure the effect of your policies on...

- the recruitment, development and retention of employees with disabilities;

- the educational opportunities available to pupils with disabilities ;
- the educational achievements of pupils with disabilities.

You are not *required* under the specific duty to gather information on other people with disabilities using your services, such as parents with disabilities and carers of children at your school, or members of the community with disabilities attending school events. However, the general duty still applies to these groups and, if you are able to collect such information, you will be in a better position to show how you are promoting disability equality for people with disabilities using the school.

Note that the process of information gathering as part of the equality duty is not an end in itself, it is just a way to enable you to make better decisions about what actions would best improve disability equality i.e. it is an *output*, not an *outcome*.

You should be looking at outcomes such as educational attainment, the numbers of people with disabilities in meaningful employment grades, and satisfaction levels, and at the sort of barriers people with disabilities face, such as inaccessible forms of communication.

Until the introduction of the Disability Equality Duty there was no requirement on schools to collect this information. Schools collect information about pupils with SEN under your schools census. However, this may not include all the pupils with disabilities at your school, for example there may be pupils who do not have SEN but have a medical condition, such as diabetes, severe asthma, epilepsy, chronic fatigue syndrome, or a mental health condition, or pupils may have hidden impairments (see page 12).

Opportunities and achievements of pupils with disabilities

If pupils with disabilities are in your school and participating in every aspect of the life of your school, how well are they achieving? You need to undertake an analysis of outcome data for pupils with disabilities, which includes...

- exam results
- accredited learning
- end of key stage outcomes
- comparative progress measured by the optional SATs
- achievements in extra-curricular activities
- broader outcomes such as those set out in *Every Child Matters*.

Your approach may differ for new pupils and for existing pupils. If you don't already gather information on disability through the admissions process, this is a good place to start. However, a number of factors can affect the response from parents:

- how parents are asked
- how parents think the information will be used
- parents' understanding of what may amount to a disability. Because it is a wide definition, it is advisable to ask a broadly cast question, for example, 'Does your child have any learning difficulty, medical condition or disability?'

Example

A school compiles and receives a substantial amount of information about their pupils. This includes information about admissions, exclusions, test scores (such as SATs), and bullying. From time to time they also record specific information about the broader aspects of school life such as participation in school trips and after school clubs.

The school realises it needs to separate out the information relating to pupils with disabilities and analyse any differences between pupils with disabilities and those without. This leads them to realise that participation on school trips and in after school clubs is substantially lower for pupils with an 'autism spectrum disorder' (ASD). The school needs to consider why this is happening, and consults with the pupils with ASD and their families to identify why they are currently not able to take part.

Encouraging Disclosure

The main reason for knowing who is disabled is to ensure that reasonable adjustments are made for those people. People with disabilities are not required to disclose a disability, though it is in their interests to do so if they need reasonable adjustments to be made for them. Pupils with disabilities, staff and parents may not feel comfortable disclosing an impairment or health condition unless they know why the information is being requested, and what impact the information gathering is likely to have for them. Some staff don't want others to know about their health condition.

There will be some people who do not know that their impairment or health condition would meet the definition of disability in the EA, for example: someone diagnosed with breast cancer may not realise that their impairment is covered by the EA.

To overcome these barriers, you should...

- provide simple information on the definition of disability in the EA
- be positive about the sort of adjustments that can be made and the benefits of these
- explain why information is needed
- reassure pupils, staff and parents about confidentiality
- ensure that the ethos of your school is conducive to disclosure.

People will feel more comfortable about acknowledging an impairment or health condition if the circumstances in which they are asked about it encourage them to believe that the information they disclose will be handled sensitively and confidentially, and used to improve opportunities and outcomes for them.

Example disclosure letters can be found in Appendix 1.

Recruitment, development and retention of employees with disabilities

Schools are specifically required to set out their arrangements for gathering information on the recruitment, development and retention of employees with disabilities. The duty applies to all those working at your school in whatever capacity and includes those who are working under a contract.

If your school employs fewer than 150 people, you are not *required* to publish this information but will still need to collect the information in order to meet the legal requirement to conduct equality analysis on employment policies and practices. You are required to publish the details of any analysis which takes place and any information used in that analysis.

Working with the local authority

Different aspects of employment may be the responsibility of your school or the local authority. This will vary according to a number of factors:

- the status of your school, for example: whether it is voluntary, community, an academy, or a free school;
- the range of functions that is delegated to your school;
- the extent to which your school buys back some functions from the local authority.

Whatever the arrangements, it is important to liaise with the local authority over the respective responsibilities of your school and the local authority. The local authority may have agreed policies with schools on phased return to work after illness, sick leave policies and monitoring. These may be relevant for staff with disabilities.

New staff

Where you do not already gather information on disability, a good place to start is the collection of information through the recruitment process. It is important to remember that applicants are never *required* to disclose a disability, and you need to take account of the points made about disclosure. Where the local authority has a role in the recruitment process, you should liaise with the authority over the collection of information.

Existing staff

You may decide to send a questionnaire to employees, at their home address. Initially such information is likely to be incomplete and imperfect. As information on staff improves, it will be important to analyse the information in respect of the representation of staff with disabilities:

- in all aspects of the work of your school, for example: teaching, teaching support, administrative support
- at all levels of seniority
- amongst those awarded Teaching and Learning Responsibility Payments
- as permanent or temporary members of staff, full- or part-time or casual staff
- in training and professional development opportunities
- in disciplinary and capability proceedings
- in harassment and bullying procedures
- as contract staff, for example: contract cleaners and agency supply teachers
- among those who take sick leave
- among trainee teachers on placement
- among those leaving the profession early

Retaining staff

Gathering information on the representation of people with disabilities within the workforce should involve an analysis of whether the appropriate reasonable adjustments are being made, and the support provided to staff with disabilities.

Becoming a disability friendly place to work and having a diverse workforce is likely to be associated with improved retention and can bring wider benefits to your school such as...

- a wider field for recruitment
- retaining the experience and skills of employees who become disabled during their working life and avoiding the costs of recruiting and training new people

- developing in-house expertise about what staff with disabilities and/or pupils may require
- providing role models for children and young people
- bringing different life experiences and new skills to your school
- helping foster good relations with all employees by showing that everyone is valued and treated fairly.

Participation of pupils with disabilities

One of the three aims of the DED is to advance equality of opportunity between people with disabilities and people without disabilities. Information must be gathered to determine the current situation, and to measure future improvement in this area. To this end, you may wish to measure...

- areas of the curriculum to which pupils with disabilities have limited or no access. Some areas of the curriculum present particular challenges, for example, PE for pupils with a physical impairment, science and technology for pupils with a visual impairment, humanities for pupils with learning4 difficulties;
- how disability issues are reflected in the curriculum;
- how pupils with disabilities participate in extra-curricular activities. Some aspects of extra-curricular activities present particular challenges, for example: lunch and break times for pupils with social/interaction impairments, after-school clubs for pupils with physical impairments, school trips for pupils with medical needs;
- parts of your school to which pupils with disabilities have limited or no access at the moment, or whether physical features of your school environment hamper access to the whole life of your school;
- how different forms of communication are made available to enable all pupils with disabilities to express their views and to hear the views of others;
- how access to information is planned, with a range of different formats available for pupils with disabilities; and
- other issues which affect the participation of pupils with disabilities, for example: bullying, peer relationships, policies on the administration of medicines, the provision of personal care, the presence or lack of role models or images of people with disabilities, in effect, all your school's policies and procedures, written and unwritten.

Careful consideration of these issues may indicate some clear priorities for your school's scheme. Other issues may need to be addressed more immediately by making reasonable adjustments to school policies, practices and procedures, for example to your school's behaviour policy.

Step-by-step guide

Taking the following steps will help you to meet your equality information obligations:

- Look at what relevant information you already have that demonstrates how you are complying with the general equality duty, including what you already publish.
- Think about what relevant qualitative data you hold that you could also usefully publish to provide a more complete picture. This could be information gained from engagement with protected groups or others.
- Put your information into a format that enables you to publish it in an accessible way.
- Read and consider the Government's Public Data Principles.
- Publish this information. Government transparency principles state that you should aim to publish data when it is available rather than just once a year.
- Identify where you have gaps in your information. These could be in relation to particular services or to particular protected groups.
- Decide what you want to be in a position to publish in the future.
- Decide at what intervals you will publish your information.
- Draw on your information (and national information) to identify your most significant equality challenges.
- Consider how you will use your information to develop and monitor your objectives.
- Consider benchmarking your performance against other relevant public authorities or national information as your basic data improves.
- Decide what steps you are going to take to fill in information gaps, including any engagement that you will undertake to do this.

Additional resources

These booklets can be found at the Inclusive Choice website on the "Books" resource tab:

- *Do you have a disability – yes or no*
- *Doing the duty overview*
- *Effective leadership - Ensuring the progress of pupils with SEN and disabilities*
- *Removing Barriers to Achievement*
- *Disability disclosure, confidentiality, and evidence in a Higher Education context - Extended Guidance Notes*
- *Ofsted Guidance for Inspectors on Self Evaluation 2011*

EQUALITY ANALYSIS

The change in terminology from 'impact assessment' to 'equality analysis' is intended to focus more attention on the quality of the analysis and how it is used in decision-making, and less on the production of a document. Equality analysis is a systematic approach to the analysis of the effects of a policy, practice or procedure on pupils with disabilities, staff and parents. You need to assess the impact of your current policies on people with disabilities, and how they further the three aims.

For each policy, you should determine if there are any unintended consequences, and also consider if the policy will be fully effective for all protected characteristics.

You are not required to follow any specific methodology or template to undertake equality analysis, but you need to be able to show that you have had due regard to the aims set out in the general equality duty.

The equality analysis requirement includes new policies and existing policies. To make the task of analysing existing policies more achievable, it is good practice to set out a timetable for this, and prioritise them.

Outcome Based Accountability (OBA)

Referring back to the section on OBA presented on page 14, remember that there are three performance measures that you could use to ensure that what you are doing is improving the lives of people with disabilities in your school…

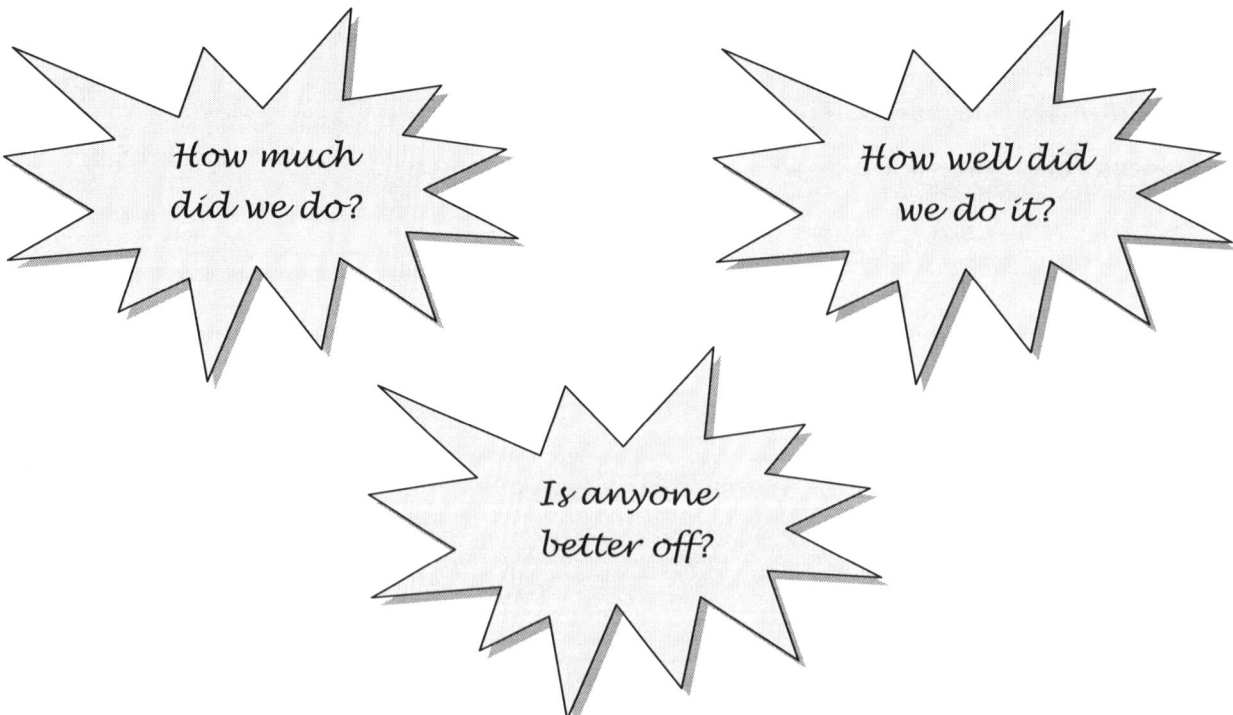

The most important is "Is anyone better off?" It is important to measure how people with disabilities are better off. Have pupils with disabilities, staff and others benefited from the proposals in your equality objectives? You should report progress "how well did we do it?" and "is anyone better off?" as these will be good ways to measure your school's success in achieving its equality objectives.

It is all very well spending a lot of time gathering data, and changing policies, but if there is no measurable improvement in the life of people with disabilities in your school, then it is all for nothing.

You should stay focused on what it is your school is trying to achieve. What will successful outcomes will look like? Is anyone better off for the changes you have made to your policies and procedures? Be careful that your equality analysis doesn't just become an academic process that just produces 'outputs' rather than measurable 'outcomes'.

Example

A school compiles its action plan with the following actions:

1. Determine how many pupils with disabilities there are at the school and create a database of what disabilities they have.

2. Determine barriers to learning for visually impaired pupils in the school.

Think about these actions. Do they result in *outputs* (i.e. some form of result that the school can use) or *outcomes* (i.e. benefits for people with disabilities)?

It is very easy to fill an action plan without considering whether anyone will actually be any better off.

Example

A teacher always dictates the homework to her top English set. One boy in the set is dyslexic, and has short term memory difficulties. When he gets home, he can't understand what he has written, and he can't remember either. Consequently, his English homework is often marked incorrect or is missing altogether.

Would your equality analysis process pick this up?

Stages of the Equality analysis process

Analysis needs to be done by the people developing the policy, not by one person or specialist team. The following steps can be taken to assess the impact of your policies...

- Make sure your colleagues know their responsibilities, know where to get the data they need and have the necessary skills.
- Examine all current policies and practices
- Screen policies and practices to determine priority
- Assess the impact/outcomes
- Explore options and make decisions
- Identify monitoring processes
- Publish the results of the equality analysis process

Like previous duties, the equality duty means taking a proportionate approach to equality analysis. This means taking an approach that is suitable to the size, resources and functions of your school, and the relevance of the policy to equality and good relations.

Equality analysis early on avoids wasting resources when a policy needs to be changed because it discriminates against certain groups. Using an agreed methodology for your analysis will help to build consistency into your work and enable you to compare progress made over time.

Base your analysis on clear information rather than on stereotypes or untested assumptions about particular groups. Analyse the effect on equality of any decisions you make about commissioning out any particular functions.

A number of public authorities have carried out an equality analysis, or impact assessment at the end of the policy development process. In some cases this has resulted in legal challenges. Undertaking equality analysis at this stage can lead to several problems:

The policy may still contain potentially discriminatory points or adverse effects on particular groups.

There may be an opportunity to advance equality that is missed, meaning that some groups do not benefit from the policy to the same extent as others.

Case precedent suggests you will be unlikely to be able to demonstrate that you had due regard to the aims of the duty at the point when decisions were being made. You may consequently be left open to compliance action by the EHRC or legal action by others.

Whatever approach you take to equality analysis, case law has established that you should keep an accurate, dated, written record of the steps you have taken to analyse the impact of your policies and practices on equality. Have you established a policy analysis procedure in your school?

Additional resources

These booklets can be found at the Inclusive Choice website on the "Books" resource tab:

- *Equality analysis and the equality duty*
- *Doing the duty overview*
- *Extending Inclusion*
- *Parental Confidence DCSF*

EQUALITY OBJECTIVES

Setting equality objectives is about planning the work that you are going to do in the next period. Equality objectives are a requirement for schools under the specific duties and they are there to help you meet your obligations under the general equality duty. The development of your objectives is likely to be one of the most significant areas of meeting your obligations under the duty, so taking time to engage genuinely but proportionately with a wide range of people on your objectives will greatly improve your duty and improve the transparency of the process.

They are not enough on their own to enable you to meet the general equality duty though. As well as being a legal requirement, setting objectives encourages an outcome-focused approach to setting challenging but measurable targets to improve outcomes for people with disabilities.

How to set objectives

You are required to consider both your equality information and your equality analysis when setting your objectives. There is also a requirement to publish details of how you engaged with people with disabilities in the development of your objectives. Views from people with disabilities can help shape your early thinking on priorities. The engagement process can continue during the process of developing objectives also.

Senior managers should be involved at this early stage to ensure that the final priorities selected will have their support. It is important that your objectives are based on sound information and analysis rather than merely being a collection of ideas from colleagues across your school, and they should address all three aims of the general duty. You are also required to show how your objectives relate to the equality information that you gathered.

When selecting criteria for choosing objectives, take into account:

- What does your information at a local level tell you about the importance of this issue?
- How significant is this equality issue?
- How will it contribute to the three aims of the duty?

- How many people with disabilities are affected by the issue? Bear in mind that it does not necessarily mean that advancement of equality is less important when the numbers in an equality group is small.
- How will delivering this particular objective improve the experiences of people with disabilities?

When you have a long list of potential objectives, review the list and ask yourself:

- Are all three aims of the general duty covered?
- What can you realistically deliver?

When you have your list of draft objectives, it is useful to engage again with the people involved in the original engagement to give them the opportunity to make comments and suggest amendments. Remember, it is a legal requirement to publish the details of the engagement you undertook when you were developing your objectives.

Try to form partnerships to help support your school in reaching its objectives. Looking beyond your own organisation when considering other support is a good way to ensure you seek other opinions when it comes to setting your equality objectives. Partnerships can be created inside your school or with other organisations such as charities, specialist schools, Parent Partnerships, and parents themselves.

Smart objectives

The specific duties require you to ensure that the objectives you set are specific and measurable, and that you identify how progress is to be measured. In order to be specific, set out clearly what policy, function or practice your objective and the outcome you seek to achieve relates to.

While it is a legal requirement to have objectives that are specific and measurable, it is helpful to follow best practice in the development of objectives that are 'SMART':

- Specific
- Measurable
- Achievable,
- Realistic
- Time-bound

Avoid vague objectives, which will not meet the criteria of SMART, such as *"we should give more attention to the access requirements of children with disabilities"*.

More details on setting SMART objectives can be found in the document "Ten Steps to SMART objectives" which can be found at the Inclusive Choice website on the "Books" resource tab.

Reviewing and publishing your objectives

You must review and revise the scheme every four years. Ideally, therefore, your objectives should cover a period of up to four years. As part of the review, check to see if your actions have led to *real* improvements for people with disabilities. It's all too easy to write lots of documents, perform lots of reviews and actions, but not actually help anybody in real life!

The review of the scheme will inform its revision - how your school sets new priorities and new action plans for the next scheme. This process must again involve pupils with disabilities, staff and parents and be based on information that your school has gathered.

After the review, a new scheme will be written. Learn from the problems encountered in the previous scheme. Don't be too ambitious. Make sure that any planned actions are likely to lead to material benefits for people with disabilities.

You must evaluate the effectiveness of the scheme and show this evaluation to your school improvement partner, and Ofsted when your school is inspected.

OUTCOME BASED ACTION PLANS

Action plans need to be sufficiently explicit to enable you to judge whether or not your targets have been achieved. Action plans should show:

- clear allocation of lead responsibility
- clear allocation of resources
- an indication of expected outcomes or performance criteria
- clear timescales
- a specified date and process for review

The actions in your plan should be prioritised to make sure that the most important ones definitely get done. Filling the action plan with lots of good-intentioned activities, and then failing to fulfil many of them is pointless.

The Outcome Based Accountability approach can provide a useful framework, or set of questions, to help schools work collectively to ensure that they are planning effectively and to know whether they are making a difference to the lives of all children with protected characteristics.

It is essential that each action includes an outcome which is designed to improve the life of people with disabilities. The emphasis should always be on identifying outcome-oriented actions rather than outputs which are easily measured but do not necessarily measure the key experiences which matter to people with disabilities.

An example action plan

Item: 1	Priority: *Medium*
Issue to address	The parents of children with disabilities may not be aware of the best way to support the learning needs of their children.
Three aims reference	Advance equality of opportunity between people with disabilities and other people.
Desired outcome	Parental engagement in their children's learning is increased to the benefit of the child.
Action to be taken	Two workshops to be conducted per year for parents of children with disabilities to provide basic advice on supporting their child's learning.
Equality analysis	Satisfaction surveys to be conducted with parents after each workshop. Follow up surveys to ascertain whether parents felt improvements have been made. Identify any outside agencies that may be needed to improve workshops. Seek parental input for this.

Responsibility	Start date	Completion date
SENCO	Dec 2011	Dec 2012

Monitoring frequency
After workshop, then two months.

Item: 2   **Priority: High**

Issue to address	Level of disability related exclusions may be disproportionate
Three aims reference	Eliminate discrimination, harassment and victimisation
Desired outcome	Eliminate high levels of exclusion for pupils with disabilities. Raising educational achievement of the pupils
Action to be taken	Reflect on levels from previous years. Review behaviour policies and implement a differentiated policy.
Equality analysis	Compare exclusion levels at the end of the year with those of previous years. Compare educational achievement of pupils.

Responsibility	**Start date**	**Completion date**
Head	Dec 2011	Dec 2012

Monitoring frequency		
In monthly review meeting		

Having a criteria on which to evaluate your action plans can really help make sure your plan will be focussed on outcomes. There are four criteria you may wish to use to test the potential value in your action plan:

- Specificity. Is the proposed action specific enough to be implemented?
- Leverage. How big a contribution will it make to improve outcomes?
- Values. Is the proposed action fair and ethical?
- Reach. Is it feasible and affordable?

An example of a good action plan is shown on page 55. Most action plans you may have seen have the subjects in columns, and each action in a row of a single table. The problem with that format is that you can't fit much text into the resulting tall narrow boxes, there is a tendency to keep things more brief than they should be, and they are rather difficult to read. The one-page-per-action format shown here ensures that each action has plenty of space to describe the issue to be addressed, desired outcomes, actions etc.

Additional resources

These booklets can be found at the Inclusive Choice website on the "Books" resource tab:

- *Doing the duty overview*
- *Equality objectives and the equality duty. A guide for public authorities*
- *Ten Steps to SMART objectives*
- *Evaluating Educational Inclusion - Guidance for Inspectors and Schools*
- *The DED – impact so far and legal enforcement*

3 THE THREE AIMS

The duty requires schools, when carrying out their functions, to have due regard to the need to:

- Eliminate discrimination, harassment and victimisation.
- Advance equality of opportunity between people with disabilities and people without disabilities.
- Foster good relations between people with disabilities and people without disabilities.

We will now cover each of these in turn to see what they mean, and present some ideas for how you could address them.

ELIMINATE DISCRIMINATION, HARASSMENT, AND VICTIMISATION

Discrimination

This refers to the discrimination defined under the EA, which is covered by the discrimination duties described on page 13. However, the DED is about your general school policies and attitudes, not about individual cases of discrimination. This element is about changing your school culture such that individual occurrences of discrimination become much less likely, with a target of entirely eliminating them.

How many cases of discrimination occur in your school every year? It is likely that you don't really know, so your first action will be to gather the required information. You may do this by counting:

- The number of parental complaints about incidents with a child with a disability
- The number of complaints from children with disabilities
- The level of disability related exclusions

To reduce cases of discrimination, your staff must be trained so that they realise when they are discriminating against a pupil with a disability. This is often not as easy as it sounds. The duty to avoid less favourable treatment in particular can be tricky to understand. It's not just the senior staff that need training in this area. Discrimination is just as likely to occur in the playground as in lessons, or when eating meals. Are your part time staff that look after the children at these times trained in their legal duties?

Your school policies should be reviewed to ensure there are none which are unintentionally discriminating against disabled or SEN children. For example, your anti-bullying or equality policy probably states that instances of racial abuse should be

Free to be me

punished immediately and strongly under defined procedures. This is a worthy intention, but what if you have a child with Tourette's syndrome who has no control over their utterances and makes a racist remark? This is a known symptom of Tourette's syndrome, and if this child is punished in the same way as a child without Tourette's then you would be in contravention of the Less Favourable Treatment duties of the EA.

This particular case may be handled with a differentiated policy, but may also require education of all pupils about disability in general, Tourette's in particular, and careful handling and explanations for the child who has been abused.

Exclusions of children with disabilities are typically 16 times more likely than their non-disabled peers (Department for Education and Skills National Statistics, *"SFR/21/2007 Permanent and Fixed Period Exclusions from Schools and Exclusion Appeals in England, 2005/6"*). Your exclusions policy is a particularly important area to ensure that children with disabilities are not being discriminated against. Are you sure that when you exclude a child that they do not have a hidden disability (see page 12). You should be particularly careful when excluding a child with a disability that all reasonable adjustments were made to prevent the incident which resulted in the exclusion, and that the reason for exclusion is in no way related to the child's disability, otherwise this is a breach of the Equality Act.

Harassment

Bullying is more prevalent than is often thought and is more so for pupils with disabilities. In a survey commissioned by the Equality Human Rights Commission in 2002, 38% of young people with disabilities said that they had been bullied at school. In a more recent survey by the National Autistic Society, 40% of children on the autistic spectrum were found to have been bullied at school.

Ofsted have placed equalities and human rights at the heart of their approach to regulation and inspection in England. The inspection framework for schools includes specific questions about:

- how schools are meeting their equalities duties
- whether there are different outcomes for different groups of children

- how schools are dealing with bullying.

Example

A primary school has recently revised its anti-bullying policy. Some key features of the policy are:

- To immediately challenge pupils using negative race or disability related language

- Implement better reporting and follow up of incidents of bullying

- Implement a range of actions, including assemblies and class work, to promote mutual respect

- Introduce a buddy system and peer mentoring as both supportive and preventative measures

The more detailed reports of bullying incidents, made under the new policy, show that pupils with disabilities are bullied much more than other children. The school decides to:

- train more buddies

- extend the buddy system to all pupils with disabilities.

As a starting point, schools need to raise awareness amongst staff and pupils of disability-related harassment. An understanding of the nature and prevalence of bullying and harassment will help your school to recognise and address it. The engagement of pupils themselves is a key feature of effective systems for combating bullying.

Disability-related bullying and harassment is not restricted to pupils. Staff with disabilities, parents, carers and other users of your school may also experience it and schools need to consider what steps they may need to take to identify and address disability-related harassment for them, too. Some ideas are...

- An initial questionnaire can be distributed to pupils and adults. The questionnaire helps both adults and pupils become aware of the extent of the problem, helps to justify intervention efforts, and serves as a benchmark to measure the impact of improvements in the school climate once other intervention components are in place.

- A parental awareness campaign can be conducted during parent-teacher conference days, through parent newsletters, and at PTA meetings. The goal is to increase parental awareness of the problem, point out the importance of parental engagement for program success, and encourage parental support of program goals. Questionnaire results are publicized.

- Teachers can work with pupils at the class level to develop class rules against bullying. Many programs engage pupils in a series of formal role-playing exercises and related assignments that can teach those pupils directly involved in bullying alternative methods of interaction. These programs can also show other pupils how they can assist victims and how everyone can work together to create a school climate where bullying is not tolerated.

Example

One year after introducing a buddy system, a primary school reviews the number of bullying incidents that are disability related. The number of incidents does not appear to have reduced significantly. The SENCO is asked to explore, with pupils with disabilities and their buddies, what is happening. The pupils are clear that they feel more comfortable about reporting incidents and that the buddy system is helping to address the problem. The school takes the view that disability related bullying was probably under-reported before. They think that the scheme is working and that it needs to continue. In addition it plans a series of assemblies to address bullying, to raise awareness of the buddy system and to stimulate a wider discussion of diversity.

A rights-respecting school not only teaches about children's rights but also models rights and respect in all its relationships: between teachers and pupils, between teachers, and between pupils.

Changing attitudes towards people with disabilities should be viewed as more than just a one time event; it must go on continually in your school. It is not a quick fix but a permanent whole school approach to the three R's:

Rights:

- The right to a childhood (including protection from harm)
- The right to be educated
- The right to be healthy
- The right to be treated fairly (which includes changing laws and practices that discriminate against children)
- The right to be heard (which includes considering children's views)

Respect: Refers to the means by which someone demonstrates regard for the worth of someone else. Respect for others requires one to treat all people as having dignity and rights commensurate with one's own.

Responsibility: Is an extension of respect. If we learn to respect people with disabilities, we value them. If we value them, we feel some responsibility for their welfare.

There is evidence through the UNICEF UK "Rights Respecting Schools" project that teaching children about their human rights can reduce bullying, truancy and exclusions, improve relations with teachers and create a calmer atmosphere for learning. The evidence is highlighted in a three-year study of the Rights Respecting School Award (RRSA), undertaken by researchers at the universities of Sussex and Brighton:

> 'In a study of thirty-one schools, researchers found that there was *"little or no shouting"* and that conflicts between pupils escalated far less frequently than they had done before the schools adopted the new approach. Fixed-term exclusions decreased in thirteen schools, stabilised in three, and five reported no exclusions'. One again there is much evidence to show that adopting a Rights Respecting approach to tackling issues such as discrimination, harassment, and victimisation can have a lasting positive effect on the whole school environment.'

Additional resources

These booklets can be found at the Inclusive Choice website on the "Books" resource tab:

- *Make them go away*
- *What is harassment on the grounds of disability*

ADVANCE EQUALITY OF OPPORTUNITY

Where you are working proactively to make reasonable adjustments for pupils with disabilities at policy and whole school level, as well as for individual pupils, you will already be doing much to promote equality of opportunity for pupils with disabilities and to secure their participation in every aspect of school life.

You can incorporate priorities from your existing accessibility plans into your scheme. These priorities may form a substantial part of your school's scheme. There will be further priorities to add in respect of promoting equality of opportunity for staff with disabilities, parents, carers and others who use your school.

Example

As part of the development of their disability equality scheme, two teachers in a primary school meet parents of children with disabilities. The parents identify school trips as a difficult area: parents are often expected to accompany their children and for the year 6 trip in particular, some of the parents say that the children resent the fact that the parent go too. The parents also feel it limits the development of their children's independence.

The information that the school holds confirms that almost invariably parent accompany children with disabilities on trips. As part of their scheme the school undertakes to re-examine their trips policy and set the following targets.

- By the next year 6 trip, they will not have to ask or expect parent to come on the trip, though parents who express a wish to come will be welcome; and

- A year after that, appropriate arrangements will be in place so that all parents can be confident that their child can go on a school trip safely without them.

In this example, the school is already making reasonable adjustments to ensure that all pupils go on school trips. It is by the active engagement of the parent and the consideration of information that schools will be able to identify further action to promote equality of opportunity.

Equality of Aspirations

Use of technology to enable schools to support pupils with disabilities

A school installed accessible software on all of their computers to assist pupils with disabilities. They provided pupils with Alphasmart word processors which have proved to be very useful with dyslexic pupils for taking notes. The school developed a more effective means of recording illness such as cancer/diabetes and epilepsy as well as severe allergies so that pupils can be properly supported both in class and during examinations.

All pupils who have disclosed a disability or an illness are risk assessed. The new Health and Safety Policy and Procedure also ensure that pupils are well supported if an emergency arises.

Interviewing new staff

It is important to be anticipatory when setting up interviews with potential new staff. Questions we should be asking ourselves are "have we given the candidate the opportunity to request for their interview to be structured differently?" Are the job application forms available in different formats? Are candidates encouraged to disclose their disability?

It may be useful to complete a table which forces you to think about what barriers there may be for people with disabilities in your school:

Curriculum	Attitudes and perception	Employment	Admissions and exclusions	Environment
Differentiated work	Promotion of disabled events	Interviewing policies	Differentiated behaviour policies	Steps and ramps
Formats of workbooks	Role models with disabilities	Time off	Encouragement of potential pupils with disabilities	Colours of walls and doors
…	…	…	…	…
…	…	…	…	…

Taking steps to meet the needs of people with disabilities

Often these steps may look very much like reasonable adjustments, but the main focus in the equality duty is on policy and whole school attitudes rather than the individual pupil, and a certain situation. Actions might include:

- additional coaching or training for pupils with disabilities, staff or parents;
- special facilities for pupils with disabilities at breaks and lunchtimes;
- a policy of interviewing all applicants with disabilities who meet the minimum requirements for a job.

Example

In a secondary school, one of the approaches to promoting positive attitudes to disability is through its citizenship and PSHE lessons. In one lesson pupils discuss the barriers that people with disabilities might face in participating in the democratic process. During the lesson a number of pupils raise questions about the representation of pupils with disabilities in the local youth parliament. A representative is delegated to discuss with pupils with disabilities and with the school council, how pupils with disabilities should be represented. The outcome is that the school:

- decides to co-opt two pupils with disabilities to the school council;
- provides a training programme for some pupils with disabilities who might stand for election to the school council; and
- plans some additional coaching for two pupils with disabilities who are potential candidates for the youth parliament.

Encouraging participation

Encouraging participation of people with disabilities may involve working with other partners to identify and address barriers. Pupils with disabilities, staff and parents will be encouraged to participate where:

- they see their peers with disabilities included and succeeding in the life of your school;
- pupils with disabilities, staff and parents are represented in senior, responsible and representative roles;
- there are positive images of people with disabilities participating.

Example

The governing body of a small primary school discusses how they might encourage the participation of people with disabilities within the governing body itself. As far as they know no-one on the governing body is disabled.

65

One of the governors knows that the grandfather of one of the pupils is disabled. The governor is delegated to ask the grandfather about the possibility of being co-opted onto the governing body.

Encouraging participation may involve working with other partners to identify and address barriers.

Example

A secondary school recognises that there are few pupils with disabilities participating in the extended day provision at the school. This provision is made on the school premises and run by the youth service. Both the school and the youth service are keen to promote the participation of more pupils with disabilities. They decide:

- the youth service will discuss with pupils with disabilities who do attend, what the service might need to do to support more pupils to attend and will explore training for all staff;

- the school will talk with other pupils with disabilities who attend the school but do not currently attend the extended day provision and will work with them to identify and remove barriers, and will talk with parents of pupils with disabilities to identify and remove barriers.

Two barriers are identified early on: transport arrangements and the provision of support for pupils with disabilities who might wish to attend. Further actions are agreed:

- the school will talk to the local authority and to parents about transport arrangements; and

- the youth service will hold an 'open evening' at the end of the extended day and invite pupils and parents from the school. In particular they want the opportunity to talk to pupils with disabilities and their parents about a range of ways in which it may be possible to support pupils with disabilities beyond the school day.

Treating children with disabilities more favourably – positive action

It is never unlawful discrimination to treat a pupil with a disability more favourably than another pupil because of their disability. This is called "Positive Action". A pupil without a disability cannot bring a claim of discrimination against them in this case. This means that you can, if you wish, lawfully provide additional or bespoke education, benefits, facilities or services, separate facilities, targeting resources or opportunities to benefit pupils with disabilities only or offer them on more favourable terms.

The Equality Act states that:

a) If you think that a pupil with a disability is experiencing disadvantage, you can take action to enable or encourage the pupil to overcome that disadvantage.

b) If you think that a pupil with a disability has needs that are different from their non-disabled peers, you can take action to meet those needs.

c) If you thinks that participation in an activity by pupils with disabilities is disproportionately low compared with their non-disabled peers, then your school may take any proportionate action to enable or encourage them to participate in that activity.

Positive action is not the same as positive discrimination. Positive discrimination means treating one person more favourably than another on the ground of that individual's sex, race, age, marital status or sexual orientation which is unlawful.

What is proportionate?

'Proportionate' refers to the balancing of competing relevant factors. A balance must be struck between the seriousness of the disadvantage, the degree to which the need is different and the extent of the low participation in the particular activity, against the impact of the action on other protected groups, and the relative disadvantage, need or participation of these groups.

You should ask yourself if the action is an appropriate way to achieve the stated aim, and if so, is the proposed action reasonably necessary to achieve the aim; that is, in all of the circumstances, would it be possible to achieve the aim as effectively by other actions that are less likely to result in less favourable treatment of others?

Example

A school has a policy of awarding a £10 voucher for those pupils with a 100% attendance record. The parent of a girl with a disability complained that the girl's absences from school were due to hospital visits connected directly to her disability, and that she should be eligible to receive the voucher, as it is not her fault that she could not reach 100% attendance. The parent requests that the girl be given "more favourable treatment" in this case.

The school replied:

"To allow any child to be an exception would put us in a very difficult position in deciding who and what criteria would allow an absence not to be considered when awarding 100% attendance award. There are simply too many cases, for example, a child with a broken arm and

having to attend a fracture clinic, a child that was particular susceptible to colds or someone that caught chickenpox, where a parent could claim similar to you, that it is not the fault of the child. We are concerned with your request for more favourable treatment for your child because we would have to be extremely careful to avoid claims of positive discrimination and will therefore not comply with your request."

In this example there would seem to be a blanket policy about how the school will reward pupils for 100% attendance. In this circumstance, it would be beneficial to differentiate the policy to take into account that pupils that meet the definition of disability would come under the protection of the EA, so it would not be unlawful to treat them more favourably than their non-disabled peers. This means that a school can offer benefits (in this case the voucher) to pupils with disabilities on more favourable terms, and this would be lawful.

The school could have approached the situation from a "positive action" perspective. Although taking positive action is optional, it is intended to be a measure that will allow schools to provide additional benefits to some pupils to address their disadvantage. Provided positive action is within the parameters laid down in the Act and meets the test of proportionality, it will not amount to discrimination under the Act. Remember it is never unlawful to treat pupils with disabilities more favourably than non-disabled pupils.

Positive action can often be a legitimate way of addressing a school's requirement to advance equality of opportunity between pupils with disabilities and their non-disabled peers.

It is common for prizes to be given to a whole class for good attendance. Without positive action, a pupil with a disability may affect the chances of the class receiving the prize. Not only could this be deemed indirect discrimination because the child cannot achieve the aim for a reason related to their disability, but it would obviously engender a feeling of resentment to the pupil with the disability. This would contravene your school's duty to "Foster good relations between people who share a protected characteristic and those who do not". Positive action in this case would avoid discrimination, and contribute to your school's public sector equality duty.

Additional resources

These booklets can be found at the Inclusive Choice website on the "Books" resource tab:

- *Access All Areas: disability, technology and learning*
- *Access to Education for children and young people with medical needs*
- *Accessible Schools - Planning to increase access to schools for pupils with disabilities*

- *Disability Equality - promoting positive attitudes through the teaching of the national curriculum*
- *Improving access for children with disabilities - early years*
- *Improving access for pupils with disabilities - LEA strategies*
- *Improving access for pupils with disabilities - School plans*
- *Improving the life chances of people with disabilities*
- *Including Me - Managing complex health needs in schools and early years settings*
- *Inclusion - providing effective learning opportunities for all pupils*
- *Inclusion of children with disabilities in primary school playgrounds*
- *Making reasonable adjustments for pupils with disabilities*
- *Managing medicines in schools and early years settings - DoH*
- *Managing medicines in schools and early years settings - Unison*
- *Maximising progress - ensuring the attainment of pupils with SEN*
- *Meeting medical needs in mainstream education*
- *Providing work placements for students with disabilities*
- *Rainbow bridge to participation*
- *Removing Barriers to Achievement*
- *Teachability - Creating an Accessible Curriculum*
- *Top tips for participation - what disabled young people want*

FOSTER GOOD RELATIONS

"What I've done is I've invited parents in, sometimes with the child, sometimes without the child, and I have walked them around the building. Quite fast, sometimes quite deliberately when there's a lot of movement going on and then I've just turned to the parent and said, 'do you think your child could cope with this?' So rather than say, 'no', I would say to the parent, 'do you think this is fair?' I think sometimes you have to let parents realise for themselves that this just isn't an appropriate placement".

This quote is taken from a real incident published in a December 2006 report by the National Children's Bureau. Attitudes such as these do nothing to help prevent the harassment and bullying of pupils with disabilities because it feeds in to the stereotype of children with disabilities as feeble, weak, not fit to be part of everyday school life and generally unable to cope in school. This SENCO is seeing the prospective pupil as the problem, pursuing reasons why the child *can't* be included. In a large secondary school where a variety of people may show prospective pupils round – head of year, deputies, etc – it is important that everyone realises the implications of seemingly innocent actions and comments. This SENCO's attitude could result in your school finding itself in a tribunal for discriminatory practices.

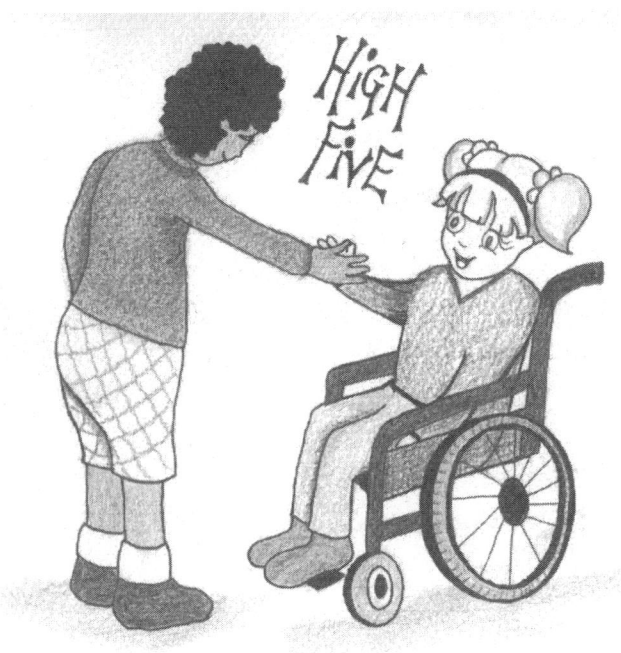

Friends forever

Improving schools' attitudes toward bullying will help us address the high numbers of pupils with disabilities that are currently being bullied in school. It is important that we work in partnership with other agencies to implement strategies to address the bullying of all children. In order to promote effective interventions towards bullying we must involve the entire school community rather than focus on the perpetrators and victims alone.

To change "hearts and minds", we must help pupils feel more comfortable about talking to and interacting with SEN and children with disabilities. How all school staff react to disability and inclusion will greatly affect how pupils will respond. Since it is teachers that generally set the example for their classes, their response pattern will prompt similar responses in their pupils, so there is a great deal that teachers and other school staff can do to promote disability in a positive light. Some examples of this might be:

- Adopting a rights-respecting approach
- positive literature and images of disability (in books and other materials appropriate for key stage)
- investigating people in history with disabilities
- guest speakers (achievers with disabilities)
- peer training
- whole school training (including lunch time staff and parent support)
- staff modelling respectful attitudes to pupils with disabilities, staff and parents
- ensuring representation of people with disabilities in senior positions in school

We must move away from the medical model of disability, which will often portray people with disabilities as victims who are constantly at risk, in danger and should be pitied.

We should promote environments where disability imagery, language and attitudes are positive whilst showing empathy and sensitivity. This will encourage reflective and tolerant behaviour from staff and pupils without disabilities. When you plan to introduce disability awareness as part of the curriculum it is important that you keep in mind key basic considerations:

1. Difference is not abnormal (what also makes us the same?)
2. Self-esteem is important
3. Classroom atmosphere is important
4. Encourage an ethos of participation, support, respect and friendships

1. Difference is not abnormal

We must provide an environment where everyone can feel comfortable talking about differences, disability, attitudes, and perceptions. Publications such as "Make Them Go Away" (which can be found on the website) provide excellent resources for schools when planning lessons on bullying that link to the curriculum. When making reasonable adjustments, consider a whole school approach towards changing attitudes as well as providing accessible environments for people with disabilities.

2. Self esteem is important to everyone.

It is what helps us to define who we feel we are and how we fit into our peer groups and society as a whole. It is important that pupils with disabilities are treated with respect and dignity. Recognition refers to the degree of attention a person or a group receives. Before one can be respected, one's existence must be recognised. If we do not show people with disabilities in roles such as judges, lawyers, doctors, bankers or teachers, if we show no disabled role models, then we can guess what degree of respect people with disabilities will receive in general or how they may come to think of themselves. Recognition is when we see the person and not the disability. It is when we recognise the individual with the disability is also "able".

As part of your curriculum you may wish to invite disabled role models to visit your school. I don't mean necessarily famous people with disabilities and certainly not exclusively "heroic" people with disabilities (the ones climbing mountains, swimming the channel etc), just ordinary people, doing ordinary things, who happen to be disabled. It is important for children with disabilities to have role models who are disabled, as well as non-disabled role models.

Part of schools' PSHE/Citizenship and SEAL should help pupils to understand the consequences of intolerance and discrimination and the results this can have on others' self esteem, and also the consequences of bullying and harassment.

The five outcomes of "Every Child Matters" are: to be healthy, stay safe, enjoy and achieve, make a positive contribution, and achieve economic well-being. These five outcomes cannot be achieved without providing children with disabilities with a solid school environment of support, respect, friendships and tolerance. We must support pupils, and tackle the idea of people with disabilities as weak, victims, and misfits.

There are some key differences between how pupils with disabilities may handle bullying and their non-disabled peers. They may…

- be adversely affected by negative attitudes to disability;
- find it more difficult to resist bullies;
- be isolated and without protective friends;
- not understand or recognise that they are bullied;
- have difficulty reporting bullying;
- struggle to remember names and details of the event;
- find it difficult to regulate their anger and emotions;

3. Classroom Atmosphere

An inclusive classroom means more than a differentiated curriculum. A positive, open and relaxed attitude towards pupils with SEN and disabilities helps create environments where both pupils with and without disabilities can form friendships. Staff should examine their own attitudes and feelings towards disability because their attitude will affect the pupils.

Equality means being together

4. Encourage an ethos of support, respect and friendships.

The way in which pupils with disabilities are depicted in school books and literature is key to building up a positive image of disability.

Positive attitudes to disability can be promoted in a variety of ways, for example:

- Start from a "Right, Respecting" standpoint

- staff modelling respectful attitudes to pupils with disabilities, staff and parents;
- ensuring representation of people with disabilities in senior positions in your school;
- through positive images in school books and other materials.

Example

A primary school reviews its reading books and recognises that there are few images of children with disabilities and adults in their current stock. They decide that they will:

- identify publishers who include more images of people with disabilities in their publications;

- promote these publishers to staff with responsibility for selecting books; and

- set a target of 20 new books with positive images, to be acquired over the following year.

Example

The History department in a secondary school reviews the content of their schemes of work for the representation of people with disabilities. They decide to adapt some of the schemes of work in Key Stage 3 to include a number of historic figures who were disabled.

The Importance of Teaching Tolerance

In our societies we all have a responsibility to change negative attitudes towards all forms of discrimination be it race, gender or disability. Schools provide us with a chance to shape young minds and produce better balanced more informed and tolerant children, even better if we can encourage and welcome any form of parental engagement with this task. To show a united, cohesive and positive whole school approach towards disability would set high standards and send out a strong message of acceptance, tolerance and respect to our community. It will also show that you are not only supportive of the Unicef Rights Respecting Schools approach, you *are* that school!

"It is everyone's responsibility to make schools inclusive for all pupils."

Materials: softball or beanbag. Time: 5 minutes

Form the class into a circle. Using the soft ball or bean bag pass it around. Whoever catches it ask them to say one thing which they can do to help. They then pass onto the next person and so on.

If a pupil needs a prompt ask them to consider the following:

What happens:

- In the playground?
- In the classroom?
- At lunchtime?
- Other pupils' attitudes?
- Staff attitudes?
- After school?

As an alternative the group as a whole can draw up a suggestion of how they think their school can support all pupils. This can be taken to the school Council for adoption by the school as a whole.

Additional resources

These booklets can be found at the Inclusive Choice website on the "Books" resource tab:

- *Altogether better*

Other Resources

- *Disabling Imagery? - A teaching guide to disability and moving image media*

  This website provides a wealth of information on how disability has been represented in moving image from the earliest days.

  www.bfi.org.uk/education/teaching/disability

4 OTHER PROTECTED CHARACTERISTICS

This book has concentrated on disability equality, since this is the most complex to implement. However, the new Public Sector Equality Duty requires that gender, race, gender reassignment, pregnancy and maternity, religion or belief, and sexual orientation are also covered.

Generally however, disability equality is the most difficult to implement. To give two pupils of different gender or different race equal opportunity is mostly a case of treating them equally. Treating a child with a disability exactly the same as a child without a disability won't necessarily give both the same opportunity. Allowing a child with a visual impairment to see the same movie as a non-disabled child doesn't give them the same opportunity to get the message of the movie. The behaviour policy on swearing may be equally applied to a child with Tourette's syndrome as a child without, but one may face a much harder task to comply with it than the other, and may suffer accordingly.

Your school has a duty to prevent and act upon any form of bullying, harassment and hate-crime. Having a whole school approach to equal rights and equal respect (see page 15) will ensure an ethos of tolerance and acceptance, and promote community cohesion. Although data evidence is of great importance to an Ofsted inspection so will the overall feeling they may get from the atmosphere in the school and attitudes of the staff and pupils.

Due regard

The duties require public bodies to pay 'due regard'. This means that the weight given to race, disability, and gender equality needs to be in proportion to its relevance. In practice this means that in order to effectively meet the duties, you will need to prioritise action to address the most significant areas of race, disability, and gender inequality and focus your efforts where they can have most impact.

When compiling your schemes it is important that you are able to provide evidence as to how your school is meeting each of the different elements of each of the duties. These are some of the questions you might want to ask when considering your equality duties to each protected group:

- Does the scheme and action plan cover all the educational body's functions including procurement and partnerships?
- Have you paid due regard to all aspects of each of the duties including your scheme and action plan?

- Have you prioritised action to address the most significant race, disability, and gender inequalities in your remit (in other words, has due regard been given?)
- Is your analysis and action plan underpinned by a good evidence base?
- If data gaps are identified, are adequate arrangements being made to address these?

Racial discrimination is not the same as racial prejudice. It is not necessary to prove that the other person intended to discriminate against you: you only have to show that you received less favourable treatment as a result of what they did.

The specific duties of the Race Equality Duty are similar to those of the DED. Schools must:

- Prepare and maintain a Race Equality Policy, with an action plan
- Involve diverse stakeholders in developing the policy
- Assess impact of all policies on pupils, staff and parents of different racial groups.
- Monitor, by reference to their impact on such pupils, staff and parents
- Implement the actions set out in the policy within three years, unless it is unreasonable or impractical to do so
- Take reasonable step to report on progress annually and review and reviews the scheme at least every three years.

Segregation

When the protected characteristic is race, deliberately segregating a pupil or group of pupils from others of a different race automatically amounts to less favourable treatment. There is no need to identify a comparator, because racial segregation is always discriminatory. However, the segregation must be due to a deliberate act or policy rather than a situation that has occurred inadvertently.

Example

A school sports club has had trouble with racial conflicts between pupils during after-school training sessions. It decides to run after-school training sessions on Tuesdays and Thursdays for black pupils and on Wednesdays and Fridays for white pupils. As separating pupils by race is a deliberate policy of the school, this is likely to be unlawful direct discrimination.

Example

A school has a uniform policy that specifies that pupils should not wear any head gear. This is likely to be indirect discrimination against a Jewish boy who wears a skullcap unless the policy can be objectively justified.

Positive Action

Remember that you can apply Positive Action. This means that you can lawfully provide additional or bespoke education, benefits, facilities or services solely to pupils with protected characteristics. Separate facilities, targeted resources or opportunities can also be supplied, and your school can offer them on more favourable terms. It is quite common for extra educational effort to be made solely for Afro-Caribbean boys, who may traditionally under-achieve academically.

Gender equality

The specific duties for gender equality state that schools must:

- Prepare, maintain and publish a gender equality scheme with action plans
- Involve stakeholders in developing the scheme
- Gather and use information on how your school's policies and practices affect gender equality.
- Consider the need to have objectives to address the cause of any gender gaps
- Assess the impact of your school's current and future policies and practices on gender equality
- Implement the actions set out in the scheme within three years, unless it is unreasonable or impractical to do so.
- report on progress annually and review and reviews the scheme at least every three years.

Example

A pregnant pupil applies to do a work placement in a garage. The school will not allow her to undertake this placement and states that this is because it would not be a suitable placement for a girl and certainly not a pregnant girl. Her pregnancy is only one of the reasons for the unfavourable treatment, the other being sex, but this is sufficient for her to make a claim of pregnancy and maternity discrimination.

The motive of the school is irrelevant, and it does not matter if the unfavourable treatment is conscious or unconscious. Pregnancy and maternity discrimination includes unfavourable treatment of a female pupil based on a stereotype whether or not the stereotype is accurate.

Draft Code Of Practice For Schools, EHRC

Example

A school holds a sports day and male and female pupils compete in separate races. This is not unlawful sex discrimination.

In considering whether separate events should be organised for boys and girls, the age and stage of development of the children competing in the activity should be taken into account.

Draft Code Of Practice For Schools, EHRC

AND FINALLY.....

A key indicator of progress on the equality duties is how far they are embedded in wider school actions like improvement plans, self-evaluation forms and the setting of performance targets for staff.

Promoting community cohesion in your school from a Rights Respecting standpoint can have a dramatic positive effect on achieving better outcomes for all protected groups.

Do you stand in the way of change or are you a driver of change in your school? Those who do not want change, who actively oppose and get in the way of positive change, can have a lasting detrimental effect on the whole school community, and inevitably this will reflect on Ofsted judgments.

"Nobody can go back and start a new beginning, but anyone can start today and make a new ending."

Maria Robinson

5 APPENDICES

APPENDIX 1: DISCLOSURE LETTERS

Dear parent,

Your support for your child's education is crucial to their progress. If your child has a disability, it is even more important that we work together so they can achieve their best, but to do this requires your school to know about the child's disability.

Your school has a duty under the Equality Act to make "reasonable adjustments" for children with disabilities. In order to make these adjustments, some information regarding your child's disability may have to be disclosed to certain members of staff in your school.

Detailed information about the nature of your child's impairments or medical information will not be passed on unless it is relevant to making reasonable adjustments. You can request that no information is passed on to others, or you can request that information is restricted to certain people. However, you should be aware that if you do this it could limit the types of adjustments your school can make for your child.

I consent to data regarding my child's disability to be passed on (please tick):

Yes ☐ No ☐ Restricted ☐

If you have ticked 'Restricted' please list below who you consent to information being passed to,
or you may like to discuss this further with your school.

Pupil's name   _____

Parent's signature   _____

Date   _____

You should be aware that even if you have asked for information about your disability not to be passed on to any other members of staff, there could be certain instances where this may still have to be done for reasons of health and safety, emergency or public policy. Information about disability is classed as Sensitive Personal data and will be processed by your school in accordance with the Data Protection Act 1998 and your school's Data Protection Policy.

Remember that your school will have to consider what other formats these letters might have to be produced in (e.g. audio tape, Braille, etc)

Dear parent,

Your school has a duty under the Equality Act to make "reasonable adjustments" for pupils with disabilities, staff, parents and others. In order to make these adjustments, some information regarding any disability you may have be disclosed to relevant members of staff in your school. Detailed information about the nature of individuals' impairments or medical information will not be passed on unless it is relevant to making reasonable adjustments.

We require your consent to pass this information to the relevant staff in order to help you get the most from your educational experience. The passing on of information is covered by the Data Protection Act and the Equality Act. We will discuss with you who we would like to tell, why we need to tell them and agree with you how much information and detail about your disability you want passed on. We will only pass on the minimum information necessary and only to the key people who need to make the adjustments you require

I consent to data regarding my disability to be passed on (please circle):

- Yes
- No
- Restricted

If you have circled 'restricted' please list below who you consent to information being passed to:

Student/parent signature ……………………………………

Name of Student/parent ……………………………………

Date ………………………………………

Staff Signature ……………………………………

Date ………………………………………

APPENDIX 2: A QUESTIONNAIRE FOR PARENTS AND STAFF

Dear Parent / Carer / staff member,

Your school has a duty under the Equality Act to make "reasonable adjustments" for pupils with disabilities, staff, parents and others. In order to make these adjustments, information regarding any disability you may have should be disclosed to relevant members of staff in your school. Detailed information about the nature of individuals' impairments or medical information will not be passed on unless it is relevant to making reasonable adjustments.

You can request that no information about a disability is passed on to others, or you can request that information is restricted to certain people. However, you should be aware that if you do this it could limit the types of adjustments your school can make for you or your child.

You should also be aware that even if you have asked for information about your disability not to be passed on to any other members of staff, there could be certain instances where this may still have to be done for reasons of health and safety, emergency or public policy

We appreciate that you may have concerns about disclosing a disability but it is important that you tell us. If you do not tell us it will be difficult for us to make the adjustments that you or your child might require to access your school. We offer many opportunities for you to discuss the nature and degree of your disability and your requirements.

Letting us know of any requirements

These are some of the ways you can let us know what support or equipment you might need:

- By telephone or by typetalk
- On this form
- In writing – by letter or email
- Through someone else such as an advocate, pare
- By talking to a member of staff

This questionnaire could be amended or could have other questions incorporated into it. It would be worth bearing in mind whether you will need to provide the questionnaires in other languages or alternative formats, to make sure that all parents and members of your school community are able to respond. Remember keep it simply and short

1. *How would you describe your impairment?*

2. *Are there any ways in which our school currently makes it difficult for you to participate in the schools life (for example to come into your school or to read information)?*

3. *Are there any ways in which your school could help you to participate in school life (for example to come into your school or to read information)?*

4.   Are there any other ideas you have about ways in which your school could improve the way people with disabilities can get the best from the school?

5.   Are there any other ways in which you think your school should involve people with disabilities in the creation of our Disability Equality Scheme?

Name (Optional): _____

Please return this questionnaire to ….

Additional resources

These booklets can be found at the Inclusive Choice website on the "Books" resource tab:

*   *Do you have a disability – yes or no*
*   *Disability disclosure, confidentiality, and evidence in a Higher Education context - Extended Guidance Notes*

Microsoft Word versions of these letters can be found on the website.

APPENDIX 3: HOW TO WRITE GOOD QUESTIONNAIRES

The following are some suggestions as to what makes a good questionnaire that is likely to be answered by as many recipients as possible.

Make it short

Your questionnaire should be as short as possible. Think about what is essential to know, what would be useful to know and what would be unnecessary. Keep the necessary, minimise the useful, and discard the unnecessary. If the information will not be used in your DES, get rid of it.

Use simple words

Your respondents may have a variety of backgrounds so use simple language. For example, "How would you classify your child's disability in terms of the impact it has on his/her academic ability?" is better written as, "How does your child's disability make it hard for them with their work at school?"

Relax your grammar

Correct grammar can alienate recipients. For example, the word "who" is appropriate in many instances when "whom" is technically correct.

Assure a common understanding

Write the questions so that they will be interpreted the same way by everyone. Don't assume that everyone has the same understanding of the facts or a common basis of knowledge. Minimise all abbreviations and jargon, and what you do use make sure you explain beforehand.

Start with interesting questions

Start the survey with questions that are likely to sound interesting and attract the respondents' attention. Save the questions that might be difficult or threatening for later. Writing questions in the third person can be less threatening than questions in the second question. For example, ask: *"How do you think parents of children with disabilities would respond to ...?"* rather than *"What do you feel about ...?"*

Avoid leading questions

Make sure the questions are phrased in a neutral way that doesn't favour any particular answer, even if you would personally prefer that response.

Balance rating scales

When the question requires respondents to use a rating scale, mediate the scale so that there is room for both extremes:

❏ *Very poor*   ❏ *Poor*   ❏ *Average*   ❏ *Good*   ❏ *Very Good*

Don't make the list of choices too long

If the list of answer categories is long and unfamiliar, it is difficult for respondents to evaluate all of them. Keep the list of choices short.

Use Closed-ended questions rather than Open-ended ones

Most questionnaires rely on questions with a fixed number of response categories from which respondents select their answers. These are useful because the respondents know clearly the purpose of the question and are limited to a set of choices where one answer is right for them.

An open-ended question normally requires written response. If there are too many written response questions, it reduces the quality and attention the respondents give to the answers.

Put your questions in a logical order

The issues raised in one question can influence how people think about subsequent questions. It is good to ask a general question and then ask more specific questions.

Test your survey

Before sending the questionnaire to the target audience, send it out as a test to a small number of people, for example, your colleagues. After they have completed the survey, brainstorm with them to see if they had problems answering any questions.

Introduction

Once a recipient opens your survey, you may still need to motivate them to complete it. The cover memo or introduction offers an excellent place to provide the motivation. A good cover memo or introduction should be short and include:

- Purpose of the questionnaire
- Why it is important to hear from the recipient
- What may be done with the results and what possible impacts may occur with the results
- Person to contact for questions about the survey
- Due date for the response

Make it personal

The proportion of recipients that will answer your questionnaire has been found to be much greater if you add a personal feature. For example, attaching a 'Post-It' note with the recipient's name and a short message will increase response rates markedly.

Dear Mrs Porter,
This will really help us provide the best services for your son. Please fill it in and return it as soon as possible.

APPENDIX 4: LEGAL ASPECTS OF DISCLOSURE

In this chapter, the term "person with a disability" is often used. For the case of small children with disabilities, this is meant to refer to their legal guardian, be that their parent or carer. This has been done to simplify the text.

Why should a school encourage people to disclose information regarding disability-related requirements? How can you ensure that it is satisfying all aspects of the law regarding confidentiality and the handling of personal, sensitive information? What evidence relating to someone's impairment should you be holding, and why?

Questions such as these highlight the complexities involved when dealing with matters of disclosure, confidentiality and evidence as they relate to people with disabilities. They also highlight the importance of having clear policies and procedures in place to avoid the possibility of finding yourself in breach of the Equality Act (2010), the Data Protection Act 1998 (DPA), and the law of confidentiality.

More information on these issues can be found in the document *"Disability disclosure, confidentiality, and evidence in a Higher Education context - Extended Guidance Notes"* which can be found on the website. Some of the information refers to the *"Code of Practice for providers of Post 16 education and related services"* which can also be found on the website. Although this may seem not to be relevant to schools, the EA treats all educational establishments the same, and a Code Of Practice is a document describing not only the law but also best practice.

Disclosure of information by pupils and parents has particular significance under the EA. The EA places the person with the disability under no obligation to disclose impairment.

Disclosure and Reasonable Adjustments

Where it appears that a school has failed to make reasonable adjustments for someone with a disability, there are two main issues to consider from a legal point of view: (1) whether your school can be said to have known about the person's impairment and (2) whether an anticipatory reasonable adjustment should have been made.

1. Did the school know?

The Code of Practice for providers of Post 16 education and related services provides that (4.20) "If a person with a disability has told someone within the school or service about his or her disability, then the responsible body may not be able to claim that it did not know."

If the school did not know, and could not reasonably be expected to have known, then it cannot be said to discriminate by treating a pupil or parent with a disability less favourably or by failing to make reasonable adjustments. However, the circumstances may be such that the school ought reasonably to have known and failure to find out about a person's impairment will not be an excuse for the school.

The Code envisages some circumstances where a pupil or parent does not directly disclose but the school 'ought reasonably to have known' that a pupil or parent is disabled through some other means. It is important that schools have procedures in place to handle these scenarios. Such a situation might result where the impairment is obvious (e.g. a wheelchair user) or information is gained from third parties, including family members. The school is also under a duty to encourage the pupil or parent to disclose an impairment.

2. Making Anticipatory Adjustments to encourage disclosure

Separate to the link between disclosure and reasonable adjustments, your school is also under general anticipatory duties to make its services and facilities accessible.

To encourage parents and staff to disclose their disabilities, encouragements can be embedded in your school's information systems. Questions can be put on application forms, reminders of your school's policies and encouragements to disclose can be circulated to parents and staff at key times in the year. Appropriate training for staff can make them easier to disclose to, and help them to handle disclosure in a way that is both useful to parents and meets your school's legal obligations.

Staff development can help staff to deal respectfully with parents with disabilities who disclose and may save staff from making elementary mistakes which could involve your school incurring liability under the EA, the Data Protection Act, and the law of confidentiality. It can also help staff to handle disclosures by ensuring that they know what resources are available, what to advise the parent and to whom they should pass relevant information about the child's impairment and support needs.

Efforts should be made to ensure that parents know that facilities exist in the school for them to disclose impairments in a way which is responsive to their sensitivities about disclosing. Establishing such a system and promoting it to parents so as to encourage disclosure may well count as an effective anticipatory reasonable adjustment.

Confidentiality, privacy and data protection

In broad outline, there are three aspects of the law which need to be considered where a person with a disability discloses to a school that they have an impairment:

The **Equality Act 2010 (EA)** provides that, where a person discloses to a school that they have an impairment, your school will be deemed to have knowledge of this and will have a duty not to discriminate against them. Where the person with the disability requests that the nature or extent of an impairment or of their disability-related requirements be kept confidential, this can have consequences for both your school and the person with the disability.

The **Data Protection Act 1998 (DPA)** is concerned with "personal data". This is defined as any information about an identifiable, living individual. The DPA also identifies "sensitive personal data" as a sub-set of "personal data". The DPA lists the types of information that are considered "sensitive personal data" which includes information about "physical and mental health". Information regarding disability is therefore likely to be regarded as sensitive personal data.

The **law of confidentiality** protects confidential information against disclosure and misuse. Traditionally, the law of confidentiality protected information disclosed within a relationship of trust and confidence such as that between doctor and patient. By contrast, recent developments in the law have laid more emphasis on the nature of the information concerned and rather less upon the pre-existence of a relationship of trust or confidence.

What are the duties of your school in the area of confidentiality?

Disability-related information is likely to be confidential in the sense that it ought not to be freely divulged without good reason. Collected by staff in the course of interactions with the person with the disability, such information may be protected by the unspoken expectation that the information will be confidential.

In addition, if a member of staff agrees to a person's request to keep disability-related information confidential, and subsequently discloses such information then, in some circumstances, they, or their employer, may have to pay damages to the person whose confidence has been broken. It is recommended that, rather than agreeing to keep disability-related information strictly confidential, staff members should make it clear at the beginning of the conversation with the person with the disability that, while they will do their best to hold the information as confidential and deal with it sensitively, they may, in certain circumstances, require to discuss the matter with other members of staff. This does not prevent them from agreeing to keep something confidential in a more limited sense. Thus it would be perfectly in order for a person with a disability to request, and for the member of staff to agree, that some arrangement be made so that other service users or other staff are not made unnecessarily aware of the nature of the person's impairment or of specific elements of their requirements.

The EA mentions that confidentiality requests by pupils and parents will be taken into account in determining reasonable adjustments. This implies that complying with such a request for confidentiality may sometimes involve making an adjustment which is less satisfactory in some sense than would otherwise be possible. Prudence dictates that your school should record that discussions took place and perhaps get a confirmation from the pupil or parent that the adjustment made, if any, was acceptable.

Your school's policies should be clear on the confidentiality of disclosure. Your school ought to have a well-thought out policy on the confidentiality of disclosures of a sensitive nature made to staff, and staff who are likely to discuss such sensitive matters ought to be well-versed in their obligations. Such a policy is likely to stress the following points:

1. Sensitive disclosures should be treated as confidential in the sense that they are not to be discussed or disclosed to anyone without good reason;

2. If a person with a disability makes a disclosure of sensitive information to a member of staff and requests that the member of staff keeps this information confidential, the member of staff should only agree to keep the information confidential to the extent that they will not tell anyone else unless they have a good reason to do so;

3. Requests for a strict degree of confidentiality, such that the member of staff is not allowed to discuss the matter with a superior, should be declined. Should the person with the disability seek one-sidedly to impose such a requirement on a member of staff, by first making a disclosure and then declaring that she regards what she has disclosed as confidential, the member of staff should point out that they will not tell anyone else without good reason but that does not mean that consultation with a superior and further disclosure if necessary is ruled out;

4. It should be explained to the discloser that, if information regarding their disability-related requirements is only known by one or a few members of staff as a result of their request for confidentiality, certain adjustments which would otherwise be available may not be able to be made;

5. In any case, all verbal discussions in which someone discloses that they have an impairment as well as requests for confidentiality should be noted in writing by staff members and, if at all possible, signed by the discloser so that a written record exists that the disclosure was made, that the discloser requested that the disclosure remain confidential and a discussion took place regarding reasonable adjustments.

What are the relevant duties of a school under the Data Protection Act 1998?

The DPA applies only to dealings with recorded personal data (i.e. personal data which is written down). It forbids the improper recording, storage and use of personal data and in particular of sensitive personal data which is at issue in the context of disability. Infringements of the DPA can give rise to civil actions for compensation, in cases where the person has suffered damage.

A school is expected to take additional precautions when dealing with sensitive personal data because of the nature of such information. The DPA requires schools to process personal data and sensitive personal data "fairly and lawfully". In order to process data fairly, the individual must be aware of what information your school holds about them, what your school intends to do with such information, and who your school will disclose it to. Therefore, it is essential that, when information about disability is disclosed, the person is told at the time that the information is collected what will be done with this information and to whom it will be passed. If this is not possible at the time of collection, it should be done as soon as is reasonably practicable after receiving the information.

In order to process information about disability fairly and lawfully, certain conditions set out in the DPA are required to be met. The most straightforward ground which allows the processing of sensitive personal data is to get the explicit and informed consent of the person with the disability.

Schools should check that their existing DPA Notification is sufficient to cover processing activities. As a requirement of the DPA, an organisation has to supply a general description of the nature of the data it holds, the processing taking place and details of the technical and organisational measures taken against (among other things) unlawful processing of personal data to a government office known as the Office of the Information Commissioner. This is known as "Notification". If a school is processing data which is not covered by its Notification, such processing is likely to contravene the DPA. In most organisation, the systems for meeting the DPA obligations and reporting requirements are administered by specialist staff, and a good deal of thought will already have gone into the matter of how staff should be instructed to deal with sensitive personal information. This may be too onerous a task for small schools, and so may be better handled centrally by the Local Authority. In that case the Local Authority must hold the data, and none of the data must be held by your school itself.

Schools should review documentation on which the personal information of people is collected. Staff should be aware that sensitive personal data should normally be gathered, stored and used only in such a way as the person has explicitly consented to; such consent needs to be well-informed and should, wherever possible, be secured in writing. Staff should be aware that processing of such data without explicit consent may incur liability for your school. Therefore, all documentation in which the personal information of people is collected, such as application forms, requests for disclosure for DED use, etc, should be reviewed to ensure they contain a data protection statement explaining what data is being collected, why it is being collected, what it will be used for and whether it will be disclosed to any third parties. Ideally, the documentation should be signed and dated by the person with the disability to show their consent to such processing.

Evidence

Evidence to justify making a reasonable adjustment

In practice, in most instances where evidence is collected, it is collected in the interest of supporting the person with the disability and to justify adjustments being made. Evidence that plays this role will often be information about aspects of a child's impairment(s) and abilities which might affect how they are cared for and handled by your school. For example, this would include assessments which establish that the child has a specific learning difficulty, reports from a doctor that certify impaired stamina, liability to infections, or dietary requirements, or specialist occupational health assessments.

In some cases, it may be appropriate also to hold evidence that the particular support or adjustment put in place will be effective in removing any substantial disadvantage which the child might otherwise face, while allowing them to meet the same fundamental learning objectives as other children.

Evidence to justify what would otherwise be discriminatory

The second reason is, in a way, the opposite of the first. The Code makes the point that 'a responsible body should not be looking for reasons or excuses to discriminate against people with disabilities...' but sometimes, unfortunately, your school will find it necessary to take actions which, in the absence of justification (such as protecting the interests of other children), would be discriminatory. Where such justification is required, it will be prudent to hold appropriate evidence in case of a subsequent claim. An example of such action contemplated in the Code is the exclusion of a child whose illness is likely to make him violent or disruptive.

Evidence collected as to the risk posed to a child with a disability, or to others, for reasons related to Health & Safety

Cases may arise where your school is under an obligation to consider the likelihood and seriousness of harm that may occur to a child or to third parties as a result of the child's health condition. This obligation arises not under the Equality Act but under the law of negligence. Since the parent of a child with a disability is likely to be in control of most of the information that will be useful in forming a view, your school will naturally seek information from them regarding the nature of this risk. This may take the form of communication from medical experts or occupational health advisers.

In extreme circumstances, where existing information suggests the likelihood of serious harm, e.g. that a child is liable to serious injury and that their illness develops rapidly and unpredictably, then this would strengthen your school's position for requiring that the child's parent produces expert evidence about the likely effects of attendance at your school on the well-being of the child before they are allowed to return.

On the other hand, as we do not ask all parents for a certificate of fitness to attend, it is important to ensure that any requirement to produce such evidence is supported by having a proportionate reason for requiring it. Asking the parent of a child with a disability to provide this evidence, in the absence of clear reasons which are both material and substantial, is likely to be discriminatory.

You should ensure that staff are aware of valid reasons for seeking evidence and refrain from requesting evidence when this is inappropriate.

Additional resources

These booklets can be found at the Inclusive Choice website on the "Books" resource tab:

- *Disability disclosure, confidentiality, and evidence in a Higher Education context - Extended Guidance Notes*
- *Data Protection Act 1998 - A Guide for Records Managers and Archivists*
- *Code of practice under the data protection act 1998*
- *Data Protection Act (1998)*
- *Do you have a disability – yes or no*

APPENDIX 5: USEFUL RESOURCES

- Skill: National Bureau for Students with Disabilities - a generally indispensable source of information on good practice for pupils with disabilities.

  `www.skill.org.uk`

- *Code of Practice for the Assurance of Academic Quality Standards in Higher Education. Section 3: Students with Disabilities.* Published in 1999 by the Quality Assurance Agency for Higher Education.

  `www.qaa.ac.uk`

- *The Data Protection Act 1998*

  `www.hmso.gov.uk/acts/acts1998/19980029.htm`

- *The Human Rights Act 1998*

  `www.hmso.gov.uk/acts/acts1998/19980042.htm`

- *Finding Out About People's Disabilities*

  A document produced by the Department for Education and Skills.

  `www.lifelonglearning.co.uk/findingout/index.htm`

- *Providing Work Placements for Students with disabilities*

  A document produced by the Department for Education and Skills.

  `www.lifelonglearning.co.uk/placements/index.htm`

- *TechDIS*
  The JISC TechDis Service aims to be the leading educational advisory service, working across the UK, in the fields of accessibility and inclusion.
  `www.techdis.ac.uk`
- Template for a school Disability Equality Scheme (*on Resource CD*)
- *Inclusive Choice Consultancy website*
  We provide many resources for parents of children with disabilities to help them with their statutory rights. You can suggest to parents of children in your school to visit our site for help.
  `www.inclusivechoice.com`

APPENDIX 6: RESOURCES FOR PROVIDING INFORMATION IN OTHER FORMATS

Braille

Braille printing machines (or Braille embossers) are still rather expensive, starting at around £1500 (e.g. Enabling Technologies Romeo Attache) and going up to over £10,000. It would be impractical for a small school to purchase one of these, but the local authority may have one.

An alternative is to use a Braille transcription service. These will take a document, print it in Braille, and post the results back to you.

There are many organisations offering this service, and a few are listed below. Typical prices are £400 per page, which is rather expensive.

Remember that Braille is not the only way to convey information to visually impaired people. In the UK less than 2% of the 1.8 million registered visually impaired people can read Braille. This is why it is important to ask people with disabilities what their preferred communication medium is, rather than making any assumptions.

Braille printing services

Braille Version	www.BrailleVersion.co.uk
Vision Support Trading Ltd	www.vstrading.co.uk
Sound Talking	www.soundtalking.co.uk
MRA Studios	www.access2print.co.uk

Text To Audio services

Although only a small number of visually impaired people can read Braille, almost all have access to tape or CD players. Although providing spoken material on these formats can be done in-house, there are commercial organisations that can do it far better for you. These can provide extra features such as tone indexes, pauses, and beeps in appropriate places to allow for information to be located easily.

Sound Talking	www.soundtalking.co.uk
Vision Support Trading Ltd	www.vstrading.co.uk
MRA Studios	www.access2print.co.uk

Text to large print services

Only 1 in 5 registered visually impaired people in the UK are totally blind. Many can read as long as the print is clear and large enough. Simply photocopying the original documents is rarely suitable. The colours may be important to many visually impaired people. Try to keep background colouring to a minimum – make sure the contrast is suitably high. Some people find a pale pink background easier to read from. Font sizes should be a minimum of 18 point.

Sound Talking   www.soundtalking.co.uk

MRA Studios   www.access2print.co.uk

APPENDIX 7: EXPECTED NUMBERS OF CHILDREN WITH DISABILITIES IN YOUR SCHOOL

The table overleaf allows you to find out the expected number of children with particular disabilities and SEN that there will be in your school, based on national prevalence rates of those disabilities. It also shows the likelihood that no pupils with that disability will currently attend your school. This can be used to determine whether your school may be overlooking these pupils, or even unwittingly discouraging them from joining your school. If you think that you have no children with a particular disability, this may inform you that you could be unaware of them, and need to better encourage disclosure.

Example of using the table

Say your school has 375 pupils. How many children would you expect to have in your school on the Autistic Spectrum Disorder? Look in the table on the ASD row. This tells us there are about 8 people in 1000 (0.8%) in society with ASD. Look further along under *"Expected number in a school of..."*, and we see that a school of 300 children would typically have 3 children with ASD, and a school of 500 would typically have 4. Therefore you should expect to have about 3 or 4 children with ASD.

You may not know of any children with ASD in your school though. What is the chance that your school could have no children with ASD? Look further along under *"Probability of having none in a school of..."*, and we can see that there is an 8% chance that a school of 300 children would have no children with ASD, and in a school of 500 children there is only a 1.5% chance that your school would have no children with ASD. In this case, it is extremely unlikely that your school would have no children with ASD (somewhere between 1.5% and 8%), so this tells you that you should be looking more closely, or that you may need to send more, or better disclosure letters.

Disability	Approx prevalence in society	Expected number in a school of...						Probability of having none in a school of...					
		100	200	300	500	700	1000	100	200	300	500	700	1000
ASD	0.8%	1	2	3	4	6	8	43%	19%	8%	1.5%	0.3%	0.0%
Tourette's syndrome	3.0%	3	6	9	15	21	30	5%	0%	0%	0%	0%	0%
Down's Syndrome	0.1%	0	0	0	1	1	1	90%	82%	74%	61%	50%	37%
Asthma	7.6%	8	15	23	38	53	76	0%	0%	0%	0%	0%	0%
Dyslexia	5.0%	5	10	15	25	35	50	1%	0%	0%	0%	0%	0%
Dyspraxia	2.0%	2	4	6	10	14	20	13%	2%	0%	0%	0%	0%
Dyscalculia	5.0%	5	10	15	25	35	50	1%	0%	0%	0%	0%	0%
Epilepsy	0.8%	1	2	2	4	5	8	47%	22%	10%	2.2%	0.5%	0%
Learning difficulties	1.5%	2	3	5	8	11	15	22%	5%	1%	0.1%	0%	0%
ADHD	5.0%	5	10	15	25	35	50	1%	0%	0%	0%	0%	0%
Mild hearing loss	14.9%	15	30	45	75	104	149	0%	0%	0%	0%	0%	0%
Severe visual impairment	0.6%	1	1	2	3	4	6	55%	40%	16%	5%	1.5%	0.2%

APPENDIX 8: BUSTING THE MYTHS

This section can be used in a class exercise. It helps address any preconceived ideas we may have about disability. We would all like to think that we never discriminate, but if we take the time to examine our deeper thoughts on disability we may find a few myths that we need to dispel and bust once and for all. This exercise would be beneficial for staff and pupils.

Myth: People with disabilities are 'not like other people' because they look, speak or behave differently.

Fact: A person's impairment is only one characteristic. We all have the same needs and rights to family life, social life, participation in society and being valued and respected.

Myth: People with disabilities are ill or infectious.

Fact: Many people live with impairment, but are healthy or active. It is not possible to 'catch' someone's impairment through contact: this fear is the result of lack of knowledge and misunderstanding.

Myth: People with disabilities can't make their own decisions because they might make a mistake.

Fact: Everyone should have the right to make decisions for themselves: even wrong ones!

Myth: You have to speak loudly to most people with disabilities: because they might have difficulty talking.

Fact: People get confused about how to communicate with a person who has a disability. They get the disabilities mixed up.

Myth: We have to talk for people with disabilities because they aren't capable.

Fact: People who take over for another person really deprive that person of a sense of self-worth and dignity.

Myth: People with disabilities don't have feelings like you - their blood is a different colour too!

Fact: People who are disabled think and feel the same as anyone, but people seem to think they should react to situations differently from other people.

Myth: People with disabilities have a poor quality of life.

Fact: This is one of the most common and damaging stereotypes, because it discourages social interactions and the development of mature relationships. People with disabilities have needs just like those who are not disabled, and they strive for a high degree of quality of life as other individuals. Society handicaps individuals by building inaccessible schools, theatres, homes, buses etc. the attitude that disability is a bad thing and that disability itself means a poor quality of life is often viewed as more disabling than the disability itself.

Myth: People with disabilities are inspirational, brave, and courageous for living successfully with their disability.

Fact: A person with a disability is simply carrying out normal activities of living when they drive to work, go shopping, pay their bills, or compete in athletic events. Access to community based long term service such as attendant care, access to buildings, public transportation, pavements, access to quality healthcare, and necessary equipment enables them to carry on the same as people without disabilities.

Myth: Disability is a devastating personal tragedy.

Fact: The lives of people with disabilities are not tragic. What often disables people is the attitudes that they encounter and the environment and the environment in which they live, work and learn.

Myth: There are people with disabilities who are 'uneducable'.

Fact: People with disabilities reflect the same range of academic ability as people without disabilities, with some achieving high qualifications and undertaking high-level jobs

Myth: Equal opportunity means that everyone is treated the same: so pupils with disabilities should not get any 'special treatment'.

Fact: Equal opportunity exists to provide all people with access to achieving their potential. The application of reasonable adjustments addresses barriers to access. It does not provide an advantage.

Can you think of any more?

APPENDIX 9. EXAMPLE SINGLE EQUALITY SCHEME

This is an example of a real single equality scheme.

2010 – 2013

I have provided this example single scheme as a starting point for you to develop or improve on your own should you need to. It should be used as a basis to discuss, develop and adapted specifically to your own community and school situation.

If you are currently in the in the process of developing an equality scheme which is founded on the human rights principles or rights respecting framework it is important that you put a paragraph in your scheme stating that you are working towards this or are already implementing this in your school.

CONTENTS

Developing the Scheme

1. Introduction

2. National and Legal Context for Equality and Diversity

3. Involvement of staff, pupils, and parents /carers

   Developing our Scheme

   Ongoing involvement

Deciding what to do

4. Equality Information

   Pupils

   Staff

   Others

5. Specific Equality Areas

   Race Equality

   Community Cohesion

   Disability Equality

   Gender Equality

   Other Equality Areas

6. Equality Analysis

7. Working in Partnership

Putting the Scheme into practice

8. Publishing the Scheme, raising awareness

9. Monitoring and evaluating the Single Equality Scheme and Equality Action Plan

11. Links with other school policies

12. Roles and responsibilities

13. Equality Action Plan

For further information, or to request this Scheme in an alternative format, please contact the Secretary.

DEVELOPING THE SCHEME

1. Introduction

We welcome the equality duties on schools, and regard these as essential for achieving the five outcomes of the Every Child Matters framework

We believe that all pupils and members of staff should have the opportunity to fulfil their potential whatever their background, identity and circumstance. We are committed to creating a community that recognises and celebrates difference within a culture of rights, respect and cooperation. We appreciate that a culture which promotes equality will create a positive environment and a shared sense of belonging for all who work, learn and use the services of our school.

We recognise that equality will only be achieved by the whole school community working together – our learners, staff, governors and parents in particular. Throughout this Scheme, 'parents' can be taken to mean mothers, fathers, carers and other adults responsible for caring for a child.

This Single Equality Scheme provides a framework for our school to promote equality, inclusion and good community relations, and to tackle prejudice, discrimination and their causes in a holistic and proactive way.

Our Single Equality Scheme is based on the core principles that its effectiveness will be determined by

- active involvement with key stakeholders, not just in developing this Scheme but also in its review and implementation
- proactive leadership
- prioritising activities that produce specific, tangible improved outcomes
- removal of attitudinal and cultural barriers

We have incorporated our individual policy for race equality, and our disability and gender equality schemes into one overarching Single Equality Scheme to create a coherent framework for promoting equality and diversity within our school. We have identified a set of priorities to promote equality, inclusion and community cohesion. Our Scheme includes a plan of action to address these priorities over the next three years.

We recognise that improving outcomes such as attendance or attainment for a specific group of pupils will help to improve our outcomes for all. Our commitment to equality is thus a fundamental part of our drive towards excellence.

2. National and Legal Context for Diversity

All schools have duties to promote race, disability and gender equality

The general duty to promote race equality means that we must have due regard to

1. eliminate unlawful racial discrimination
2. promote equality of opportunity
3. promote good relations between people of different racial groups.

The general duty to promote disability equality means that we must have due regard to

1. promote equality of opportunity between people with disabilities and other people
2. eliminate unlawful discrimination
3. eliminate disability- related harassment
4. promote positive attitudes towards disabled people
5. encourage participation by people with disabilities in public life
6. take steps to take account of peoples' disabilities, even where that involves treating people with disabilities more favourably than other people.

The disability equality general duty reinforces the reasonable adjustment duties of the Equality Act. In particular, it complements, and in some cases overlaps with, the anticipatory duty to make adjustments.

The general duty to promote gender equality means that we must have due regard to

1. eliminate unlawful discrimination and harassment and
2. promote equality of opportunity between men and women.

This Scheme demonstrates our response to both the general and specific duties.

Schools have a duty to promote community cohesion, developing good relations across different cultures, ethnic, religious and non religious and socio-economic groups. There are no statutory requirements for schools to have a policy or action plan for promoting community cohesion. However, we have incorporated our priorities into our Single Equality Scheme and Equality Action plan to make it easier to monitor our progress and performance in meeting the requirements of this duty.

3. Involvement of staff, pupils, and parents

a) Developing our Scheme

The involvement of a diverse group of people has been instrumental in shaping our Single Equality Scheme and Equality Action Plan. We have striven to involve the full diversity of our school and community, recognising that people who share an aspect of their identity in relation to race, disability, gender, age, sexual orientation and religion or belief are best placed to identify key issues for us to address.

A working party of staff and governors, representing parents and the community, has developed our scheme and a staff survey was carried out to gather information.

A summary of the scheme has been shared with parents and the full scheme has been published on the school website.

Any priorities raised by involved parties, will be addressed within this scheme.

b) *Ongoing involvement*

We have strategies in place to promote the participation of pupils in decision-making and in making a positive contribution to school life. We will embed equality and inclusion into these strategies so that learners from diverse backgrounds are involved in shaping provision and improving practice.

We ensure that outcomes from these involvement activities are acted upon by the school's senior leadership team.

DECIDING WHAT TO DO

We will collect a broad range of qualitative and quantitative information to monitor our policies and practice and to demonstrate our progress in equality, inclusion and community cohesion. Our single equality approach helps us to more effectively monitor our progress and performance, as our pupils and staff may face more than one barrier to achieving their full potential.

Equality Information

a) *Pupils*

We collect the following information with regard to race, gender and disability:-

- admissions
- attendance
- achievement and progression
- participation in the student council
- take up of extended school provision and extracurricular activities
- other equality information for example complaints and incidents of race, gender discrimination or bullying

We have identified the following priorities from evaluation of this information...

- We continue to monitor and address the gender gap in achievement with particular regard to boy's attainment at the higher levels in reading and writing.

- We will endeavour to provide a greater variety of after school sports clubs, which we hope will encourage greater participation by girls.

We will ensure that the information we gather will be used to promote equality by embedding the evaluation of performance data, disaggregated by race, disability and gender, within the school self evaluation report.

b) Staff

We collect the following information with regard to race, gender and disability...

- Staff recruitment, retention
- Continuing Professional Development
- Promotion
- Outcomes of appraisals and performance review processes
- Exit interviews of employment (views of employees, equality –race, disability & gender)

We will ensure that the information we gather will be used to promote equality by embedding the evaluation of performance data, by race, disability and gender, within the school self evaluation report.

6. Specific Equality Areas

This section of our scheme highlights what we have already achieved for specific aspects of equality, and further action that we intend to take

Race Equality

What we have already achieved:

- Although not solely unique to this particular equality issue, the school believe that the work it does to identify and tackle equality-related issues is aided by the strong analytical skills which senior staff possess.
- The school complies with the County procedures regarding the reporting of racist incidents. The school is pleased to report that in the last three years there has been a nil return in respect of this.
- The school completes a rigorous analysis of national RAISEonline data, annually. The school is pleased to report that children from ethnic minorities within the school achieve as well as children from the ethnic majority. The analysis of the RAISEonline data also shows that children from ethnic minorities achieve above the national average in all subjects in comparison to children from similar ethnic groups.
- The school is successful in promoting good relations between people of different racial groups through its implementation of the Philosophy for Children (P4C)

programme, the use of SEAL materials within the PSHCE curriculum and also Circle Times within the school.

- Whilst the community within which the school sits is predominantly of one ethnic background, the school complies with the County Equal Opportunities Policy when recruiting new staff.

We want to do more by:

Extending the use of P4C sessions into the Foundation Stage.

We want to/are working towards implementing the UNICEF Rights Respecting school framework. A "Rights Respecting School" is one where all sections of the school community know about and value the UN Convention on the Rights of the Child and everyone uses the language of rights, respect and responsibility.

Our school is working towards improved engagement and consultation between school and parents as this would help to identify need and address equality-related issues at an earlier point.

The school is working towards promoting English language support in order to ensure that we provide better support for parents and pupils for our diverse ethnic minority population in school.

b) Disability Equality

If you think that you have no staff, pupils or parents with disabilities, remember hidden impairments which might not be immediately obvious.

What we have already achieved:

Using current published Accessibility Plan provided the following to enable equality of opportunity:

- Provision of information regarding the curriculum and the school environment, published on the school's website together with the fact that this information can be provided upon request in a variety of formats
- Provision of a disabled parking space and ramp to allow access to the main school hall
- Dropped kerbs and ramps around the school site to improve ease of access as promoted through the school's Travel Plan together with the fact that this information can be provided upon request in a variety of formats
- We believe that all children are entitled to receive a broad, balanced and relevant curriculum. Inclusion is viewed as an important part of our ethos and we value all children and their families, whatever their individual needs.
- All teaching and learning takes account of our inclusion principles and every member of the school community is expected to promote and demonstrate

inclusive behaviour. All staff are responsible for the implementation of these principles and are supported and have access to a range of advice and resources to support these.

- The school tracks all children throughout the school to ensure that they are supported, planned for, and able to reach their full potential.
- Staff received or plan to receive up to date training in the EA
- Continue to work with outside agencies
- Building on parental involvement

We want to do more by:

Forming more partnership with outside agencies such as sports colleges, clubs groups or other schools. The school realises the importance of having a transparent partnership with the local authority, disability experts, staff, parents and pupils.

Building trust with parents so that we can improving and understanding the learning needs and aspirations of pupils with learning difficulties or disabilities.

Providing role models to highlight attainment and success to dispel stereotyping and images of disability and achievement. The school wants to continue to work with breaking down stereotypical attitudes among local training providers to cater for pupils with complex needs.

The school will continue working within an Outcome Based Accountability (OBA) framework. OBA makes a careful distinction between *outcomes* and *outputs*. This is important because measuring success on the basis of outputs alone can be misleading.

c) Gender Equality

What we have already achieved.

- The school is successfully closing the gap between the attainment of girls and boys at Level 3 in reading. It has done this through curriculum design, the purchase of additional nonfiction reading material and the implementation of the Read, Write Inc. synthetic phonics programme
- The school complies with the County Equal Opportunities Policy when recruiting new staff
- The school benefits from having teachers of both genders despite the fact that most recently, applications have been predominantly, if not totally, female dominated. The fact that the school has been able to recruit a male teacher has meant that we are able to offer a positive role model to boys throughout the school.
- The provision of the school's science and arts clubs, has seen an equal take up of both genders

We want to do more by:

The school is committed to revitalising the PE department to ensure equality of opportunity and all-round better provision has been a key success factor. Forming partnerships with outside sport college and the recruitment of staff from the sport college has also been key to increasing pupil participation and reducing stereotyping in sport.

Inviting gender specific role models in sport to school has also helped to dispel myths about achievement and gender in sport.

In terms of barriers we have been identifying staff attitude and funding as two key issues. We are in the process of implementing new staff training with the support of the sport college. We are tackling individual staff attitudes and monitoring progress in this area.

Funding was a considerable barrier at the beginning of initiative as financing was needed for the sport college partnership and to pay new PE teachers. We have been working towards absorbing this cost – largely through funding and natural wastage. Although funding is an ongoing concern for future plans and consistency.

Attempt to provide an after school sporting activity, which will appeal more equally to both boys and girls.

d) Community Cohesion.

Promoting understanding of the school's context:

- Home visits for all children as they start school
- Governors attend 2009 FGB County community cohesion training

Contrasting the school with the local community

- Children investigate the local area through visits to the local shops, trips to the local secondary and junior school, trip to Sainsbury's, Christmas visit to the local sheltered housing accommodation

Plans to promote community cohesion:

- Contrasting other religions through curriculum planning such as Diwali celebrations in year two and Chinese New Year in Foundation stage. Year One study aspects of Judaism and its comparison with Christianity.
- Weekly French classes for years one and two
- Support of international charities such as the annual shoebox appeal, Save the children Plumpy Nut Appeal, Children in Need and Send a Cow.
- Children wanting to respond to the recent Haiti Disaster Appeal.
- African Drumming workshop.
- Visit from a representative for Guide Dogs for the Blind.
- Use of Espresso to view and discuss the weekly national and international news bites.

Ensuring we get on well together:

- Having respect for different viewpoints - P4C work, school council, circle time
- Recognising commonalities - RE planning, PSHCE planning, P4C work
- Advocacy skills - children encouraged to take responsibilities throughout the school e.g. Playground Carers

We want to do more by:

- To promote global community cohesion, the school wishes in the future to create links with another school in a different country, possibly via the internet.
- The school will continue to review its curriculum planning, to ensure links with multiple cultures.

We are working towards implementing the UNICEF Rights Respecting school framework. A "Rights Respecting School" is one where all sections of the school community know about and value the UN Convention on the Rights of the Child and everyone uses the language of rights, respect and responsibility. The strong emphasis on the UN Convention on the Rights of the Child highlights the importance of respecting the rights of others and of personal and collective responsibility.

7. Equality Analysis

We will carry out equality analysis on our policy and practice which will cover all aspects of equality: race, disability, gender (including gender identity), age, sexual orientation, religion and belief. We will look for ways to improve practice as well as ways to eliminate discrimination and harassment. We have a programme of carrying out impact assessments on our existing policies and practice and we will build the equality analysis process into all new policy development and decision making activities.

We hope to appoint a nominated governor to lead this process. (Have your governors had training in this? See www.inclusivechoice.com *for training course)*

8. Working in Partnership

We recognise that achieving equality, inclusion and good community relations involves working effectively and in partnership with others, including parents, community groups and local organisations.

- Letters are sent to parents via the children, as are newsletters. The website is also used to publish information and shared policies (don't for get to think about the format of letter and website to make sure they are accessible where possible)
- Is your school involved in any partnership, which forms links with the community Does your Governing Body includes representatives from staff, parents, the Local Authority and the community?

PUTTING THE SCHEME INTO PRACTICE

9. Publishing the Scheme, raising awareness

We recognise that our Scheme is a public document that should be available to any interested stakeholder. We will promote and publish our Scheme by:

- Placing it on our website
- Making it available on request
- Providing a summary in our prospectus, including our vision and key priorities
- A copy of the summary will be sent to all parents and staff
- At the time of staff induction, a copy of the scheme will be made available to all new staff
- Where appropriate, other service providers will be provided with a summary of the scheme.

10. Monitoring and evaluating the Single Equality Scheme and Equality Action Plan

We will regularly monitor and evaluate the implementation of our Single Equality Scheme and Equality Action Plan. We will report annually on our progress and performance. Our annual report will be shared with Governors and our School Improvement Partner. A summary will be provided for parents and published in our prospectus and in the Summer Term Governors' newsletter.

Both will explain how the full report can be obtained. We will inform staff and learners of our progress. The school's nominated governor will lead this process.

The findings of our annual report will be used to update the Equality Action Plan and inform subsequent Single Equality Schemes.

We want this Scheme to be a 'whole organisational' document that drives forward equality and achieves improved outcomes. We will therefore ensure that the Equality Action Plan is an integral part of our School Improvement Plan, and as such, our progress will have regular oversight by the senior leadership team and the governing body

We will formally review, evaluate and revise this Single Equality Scheme and Equality Action Plan every three years, to set new priorities and identify new actions. This process will again involve staff, learners, parents and governors who reflect the full diversity of the school community.

11. Links with other school policies

School policies that link with, and have informed this Scheme include:

- Inclusion Policy
- SEN Policy

- Racist Incidence Policy
- Anti-Bullying Policy
- Pay Policy
- Admissions Policy

12. Roles and responsibilities

The governing body will

- Monitor the implementation of the Scheme and Action Plan to check progress and assess impact on staff, learners and parents
- Ensure that all governors are aware of their legal responsibilities under equality legislation
- Receive and discuss regular equality reports on progress and performance
- Monitor achievement of equality targets
- Check that implementation of the Scheme and Action Plan achieves improved outcomes for people who share an aspect of their identity in relation to race, disability, gender (including gender identity), age, sexual orientation, religion and belief
- Has the governing body had any training in any of these areas?

The head teacher will

- Provide proactive leadership to create a community that recognises and celebrates difference within a culture of respect and cooperation
- Ensure staff, pupils, parents /carers and any other interested stakeholders are aware of this Scheme and their roles and responsibilities in implementing this Scheme
- Monitor to ensure effective implementation of the Scheme and Action plan
- Provide regular reports for governors on progress and performance
- Allocate appropriate responsibilities, and provide suitable training and development for staff to implement this Scheme

The senior leadership team will

- Drive forward implementation of the Scheme and Action Plan
- Support staff to carry out their role in implementing this Scheme
- Provide effective leadership on equality, inclusion and community cohesion
- Ensure the Scheme is successfully promoted
- Respond in a timely and appropriate manner when dealing with any incidents or issues of discrimination, harassment or victimization

All staff will

- recognise that they have a role and responsibility in their day-to-day work to
  - promote equality, inclusion and good community relations

111

- challenge inappropriate language and behaviour
- tackle bias and stereotyping
- respond appropriately to incidents of discrimination and harassment and report these

- highlight to the senior leadership team any staff training or development that they require to carry out the above role and responsibilities

All staff will also ensure that pupils are encouraged to

- recognise that they have a role and responsibility to themselves and others so that they understand and are able to
  - promote equality, inclusion and good community relations
  - challenge inappropriate language and behaviour
  - tackle bias and stereotyping
  - work to promote anti-bullying strategies
  - respond appropriately to incidents of discrimination and harassment and understand the action needed to report these

Further information on the requirements of equality legislation for schools can be found at www.governornet.co.uk and www.equalityhumanrights.com.

Action plans

These action plans are for a Disability Equality Duty. The format and principle behind them can be used for race, gender, and the other protected characteristics also. They should reflect the intentions that you detailed in the body of the scheme above.

This action plan has priories of "high", "medium", and "low". You may like to add more granularity and have priorities from 1 to 10 or such-like.

In the row headings, you can see an item "DED reference". This has been put in to maintain focus on the three aims which form our outcomes. Please remember there is a difference between *outputs* and *outcomes*. Outputs are the results of some work, whereas outcomes must benefit the target recipient.

Year: 2012	Item: 1	Priority: *High*
Issue to address	The level of exclusions of children with disabilities and SEN may be disproportionate to their prevalence in society. Some excluded children may have disabilities that we are currently unaware of, and that we should have taken into account before excluding them.	
Three aims reference	Eliminate discrimination	
	Advance equality of opportunity between people with disabilities and non-disabled	
Desired outcome	No pupil with a disability should be disciplined due to a situation which arose because of their disability. *This is no excuse for bad behaviour not related to their disability however.*	
Action to be taken	Establish DES Steering Group. A representative group of children with disabilities and adults is in place to lead and review the DES. The behaviour policy shall be amended to ensure that any disciplinary action, and especially exclusions, is preceded by an investigation into the disability	
Equality Analysis	All disciplinary events are logged. This log is examined every month to ensure that the investigation into the disability status for the pupil has been completed satisfactorily.	

Monitoring frequency	Responsibility	Start date	Completion date
Monthly	Deputy head		

Year: 2012	Item: 2	Priority: *Medium*
Issue to address	Recruitment, retention and professional development of staff with disabilities	
Three aims reference	Promote equality of opportunity between people with disabilities and other people Eliminate discrimination, harassment and victimisation	
Desired outcome	Equality of opportunity for staff with disabilities with respect to their recruitment, retention, and professional development.	
Action to be taken	Put in place our commitments necessary for the awarding of the Two Tick symbol from Jobcentre Plus. Apply to Jobcentre Plus for the Two Tick mark. Work with LA to establish disability population of school staff. All job adverts must specifically state that applicants with disabilities are welcomed.	
Equality Analysis	Number of applicants with disabilities that applied for any job vacancies in the year.	

Responsibility	Start date	Completion date
Head	Jan 2007	Dec 2007

Monitoring frequency		
Yearly		

Year: 2012	Item: 3	Priority: Medium
Issue to address		Personal development, educational attainment and progress of pupils with disabilities
Three aims reference		Advance equality of opportunity between people with disabilities and people without disabilities
Desired outcome		The educational achievement of pupils with disabilities should be at least equal to that of other pupils, after taking into account the potential of that child and the type and level of their
Action to be taken		Ensure our methods for recording educational results are cross-referenced with the disability status of the child.
		Plan additional data gathering measures to ensure we have as full information as possible as to the disability status of all our pupils.
Equality Analysis		For all pupils with disabilities, review their educational achievements and ask ourselves "could this pupil have achieved more if any other reasonable adjustments had been put in place?".

Responsibility	Start date	Completion date
Class teachers		

Monitoring frequency		
End of each term		

Year: 2012	Item: 4	Priority: Low
Issue to address	Policy, Leadership and Management. Ensure all school policies are non-discriminatory. Improve information gathering and analysis techniques	
Three aims reference	Eliminate discrimination, harassment and victimisation	
Desired outcome	All school policies should be differentiated if required to ensure people with disabilities are not discriminated against.	
Action to be taken	Establish process of Equality Analysis for new policies. All existing policies to be reviewed. We understand that the number of policies means that we cannot expect to re-write them all in one year. We will therefore prioritise them first, and deal with them at a reasonable rate.	
Equality Analysis	Review all new and altered policies and discuss whether they are suitably differentiated.	

Responsibility	Start date	Completion date
Deputy head		

Monitoring frequency		
Monthly		

Year: 2013	Item: 1	Priority: *High*
Issue to address	The image of pupils with disabilities, and the attitudes of their peers and teachers towards them can be improved.	
Three aims reference	Foster good relations between people with disabilities and people without disabilities.	
Desired outcome	Identify learning opportunities in PSHE; extend audit to 'core' curriculum areas.	
Action to be taken	PSHE/Citizenship curriculum review	
Equality Analysis	Questionnaires to be designed for all pupils with carefully crafted questions to identify their true attitudes towards their fellow pupils who are disabled.	

Responsibility	Start date	Completion date
Head		

Monitoring frequency		
End of each term		

Year: 2013	Item: 2	Priority:
Issue to address		Gender equality – the curriculum.
Three aims reference		Eliminate unlawful discrimination, Promote equality of opportunity.
Desired outcome		More girls will apply to undertake courses traditionally dominated by men, and more boys will apply to undertake courses traditionally dominated by women
Action to be taken		Review the content of teaching materials to ensure that they do not include gender stereotypes. Promote alternative choices of courses throughout the school.
Equality Analysis		Courses are being taken bya more even mix of genders.

Monitoring frequency	Responsibility	Start date	Completion date
End of each term	Class teachers		

Year: 2014	Item: 1	Priority: *Medium*
Issue to address	Race equality, ethnic and cultural diversity are promoted and racism and discrimination are challenged through learning in all areas of the curriculum	
Three aims reference	Eliminate unlawful racial discrimination, Promote equality of opportunity, Promote good race relations	
Desired outcome	Pupils have equal access to the mainstream curriculum, by taking account of their individual cultural backgrounds and linguistic needs.	
Action to be taken	Review curriculum policies and schemes of work. Purchase resources promoting equality. Invite individuals to speak to pupils about religion/race	
Equality Analysis		

Monitoring frequency	Responsibility	Start date	Completion date
End of each term	Class teachers		

Guidance on using the example Equality Scheme Action Plans

The actions identified in this example action plan are linked to the Equality and Human Rights Commission guidance 'Schools and the Disability Equality Duty in England and Wales', which can be found on website. You should refer to the EHRC guidance to get the most from this example plan.

The actions identified in the first year (2012) are linked to elements of the general duty, to the eight 'functions' of school life (Policy, Leadership and Management, Curriculum, Teaching and Assessment, Admissions, Attendance, Discipline and Exclusion, Pupils – Personal Development, Attainment and Progress, Attitudes and Environment, Parents, Governors and Community Partnership including Extended Services, Staffing – Recruitment, Training and Professional Development, Pupil Voice and Participation), and to your school's Accessibility Strategy. The example actions reduce in the second year and third year (2013 and 2014) because actions in subsequent years should be informed by work done previously. By the end of the first year you may have decided on more actions for subsequent years.

To put these actions into practice you will need to do some more detailed, short-term planning with an input, where appropriate, from your participation group.

Note that this scheme is only an example. Your priorities will be different, and will depend on consultation with your whole school team.

APPENDIX 10: MORE RESOURCES

These documents can be found on the website:

- Access All Areas: disability, technology and learning
- Access to Education for children and young people with medical needs
- Accessible Schools - Planning to increase access to schools for pupils with disabilities
- Altogether better
- Code Of Practice for schools
- Code of Practice for Services, Public Functions and Associations
- Code of practice under the data protection act 1998
- Data Protection Act (1998)
- Data Protection Act 1998 - A Guide for Records Managers and Archivists
- Disability Discrimination Act 1995
- Disability Equality - promoting positive attitudes through the teaching of the national curriculum
- Disability disclosure, confidentiality, and evidence in a Higher Education context - Extended Guidance Notes
- Disable parents involvement in their children's education - an examination of good practice
- Do you have a disability - yes or no
- Doing the duty overview
- Duties and definitions
- Early years and the Disability Discrimination Act
- Effective leadership - Ensuring the progress of pupils with SEN and disabilities
- Equality Act (2010)
- Equality Act (2010) - Explanatory Notes
- Equality Act (2010) - What do I need to know - Disability quick start guide
- Equality Act (2010) easy read
- Equality analysis and the equality duty
- Equality objectives and the equality duty. A guide for public authorities
- Evaluating Educational Inclusion - Guidance for Inspectors and Schools
- Extending Inclusion
- Improving access for children with disabilities - early years
- Improving access for pupils with disabilities - LEA strategies
- Improving access for pupils with disabilities - School plans
- Improving the life chances of people with disabilities
- Including Me - Managing complex health needs in schools and early years settings
- Inclusion - providing effective learning opportunities for all pupils
- Inclusion of children with disabilities in primary school playgrounds

- Involving people with disabilities
- Make them go away
- Making reasonable adjustments for disabled teachers (NUT)
- Making reasonable adjustments for pupils with disabilities
- Managing medicines in schools and early years settings - DoH
- Managing medicines in schools and early years settings - Unison
- Maximising progress - ensuring the attainment of pupils with SEN
- Meeting medical needs in mainstream education
- Meeting the needs of teachers with disabilities (NUT)
- Ofsted Guidance for Inspectors on Self Evaluation 2011
- Parental Confidence
- Parental Confidence DCSF
- Parents with disabilities and schools - barriers to parental involvement in children's education
- Principles of good practice in involvement
- Promoting Disability Equality in Schools
- Providing work placements for pupils with disabilities
- Rainbow bridge to participation
- Removing Barriers to Achievement
- SEN Code Of Practice
- Supporting parents with disabilities
- Supporting parents with disabilities' involvement in their children's education
- Teachability - Creating an Accessible Curriculum
- Ten Steps to SMART objectives
- The DED - impact so far and legal enforcement
- Toolbag for supporting disabled teachers
- Top tips for participation - what disabled young people want
- What equality law means for you as an education provider - schools
- What is harassment on the grounds of disability

EHRC documents

There is a set of five booklets published by the Equality and Human Rights Commission that explain the new duty in detail. They can be downloaded from the EHRC website at www.equalityhumanrights.com

The documents are:

1. The essential guide to the public sector equality duty
2. Equality analysis and the equality duty. A guide for public authorities
3. Engagement and the equality duty. A guide for public authorities
4. Equality objectives and the equality duty. A guide for public authorities
5. Equality information and the equality duty. A guide for public authorities

INDEX

The Equality Act for Educational Professionals

A simple guide to disability Inclusion in schools

By Geraldine Hills

Do you know what your school's strengths are in inclusion? Are you building on them? Is your school positive about inclusion, and does it show? What role are you playing in the successful inclusion of SEN and disabled pupils?

These questions should make you think about what part you play in the successful inclusion of pupils with disabilities.

This highly practical resource:

- Discusses 'reasonable adjustments' and 'less favourable treatment' which are at the heart of the Equality Act (2010), in ways that will encourage all members of staff to feel confident that they are correctly implementing its requirements.

- Shows how 'less favourable treatment' and 'reasonable adjustments' apply to admissions, exclusions, handling of medicines and school trips through worked examples and case studies.

- Takes readers through the process of an alleged act of discrimination against a school, and how it may be resolved, up to and including the SEND tribunal process.

The author brings a wealth of experience to this topic, both as a parent of a child with disabilities, and as an experienced trainer in equality legislation and inclusion.

"A definite must for SENCOS."
Urmston Junior School

"A good insight into process of tribunal and what the Equality Act means."
Team Leader, St Paul's CE Primary School

"A much needed resource in supporting schools, centres, day nurseries and community childcare provision to understand the complexity of the issues surrounding SEN... A valuable tool."
Gerri Ross – Head of Old Moat Sure Start Children's Centre, UK

"Straightforward and easily accessible...I would recommend this book to undergraduates and professionals alike who have an interest in ensuring that the rights of disabled children are upheld."
Dr Craig Blyth, School of Education,

www.routledge.com/teachers

INSET Training

Courses in the Equality Act and the Equality Duty
are available from Geraldine Hills at Inclusive Choice

Inclusive Practice In Schools

This course trains all school staff in the Equality Act and what it means for your school. Researching all your legal requirements is hard - this course makes it easy for you. We will unpick the issues with you and explain in simple terms exactly what you need to do to comply with the EA.

"Absolutely brilliant, really useful course. Will definitely be implementing resources, etc"
Manchester Communication Academy

"Everything simple, informative, and relevant. All brilliant. Best course in ages! Thank-you"
St Mary's CE Primary, Moss Side

The Disability Equality Duty for schools

This course trains heads, teachers, and SENCOs in the requirements of the Disability Equality Duty, preparing the school's Disability Equality plans and information to publish, and the day-to-day successful running of the duty.

"An outstanding course, an outstanding trainer! Thank-you Geraldine!"
Levenshulme High School

"It's a long time since I've been on a course that was as useful as this. Excellent overview and great specific examples to help me get going."
Newall Green High School

See www.inclusivechoice.com for more details

07547 470265   enquiries@inclusivechoice.com